AUTHOR

DOBSON. Bob

CLASS

M66

TITLE

a 30118 057090551b

Landy Publishing have also published:-

BLACKBURN & DARWEN A CENTURY AGO
BURY A CENTURY AGO
WIGAN A CENTURY AGO
LANCASTER A CENTURY AGO
BLACKPOOL & FLEETWOOD A CENTURY AGO
CHORLEY A CENTURY AGO
IN LANCASHIRE LANGUAGE
VALLEY VERSES
POLICING IN LANCASHIRE
THE BLACKBURN SAMARITAN
BITS OF OLD BLACKBURN
PRESTON A CENTURY AGO
PRESTON PAST & PRESENT
ANNALS OF TRAWDEN FOREST

Bob Dobson compiled *"Clattering Clogs"*, published by Dalesman Publishing but now out of print.

Concerning Clogs

Bob Dobson

Landy Publishing
1993

Concerning Clogs was originally published in 1979 by Dalesman Publishing, and is republished with their permission.

ISBN: 1 872895 13 1

Printed and bound by Galava Printing Company Limited, Nelson, Lancashire

Contents

Cover illustration by Barbara Blundell

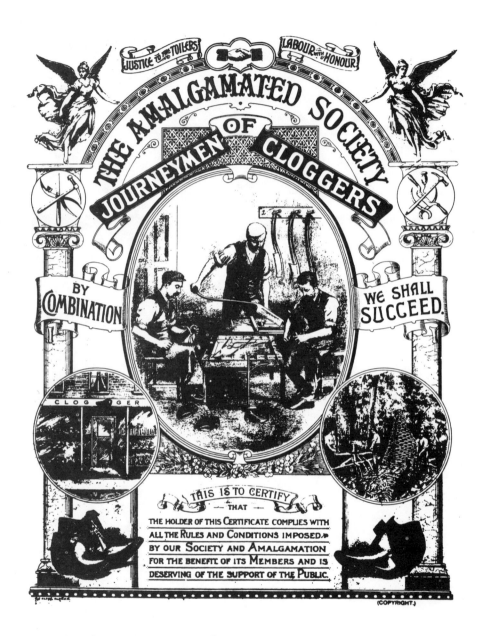

A trade union certificate of past years. Photo courtesy of the North West Museum Services Unit, Blackburn.

Introduction

I wrote this book over twelve years ago after researching on clogs for five years, and after being interested in them (as part of Lancashire culture) for almost thirty years. I felt then - and the feeling has not weakened - that clogs are an integral part of the history of Northern England. There hadn't been any proper book published which was devoted to clogs, so I decided to remedy this.

My interest in clogs started when I lived with my grandma and clogs were part of everyday life. This book was, and is, a tribute to her and to all grandmas.

I decided to republish the book just as it was, with the addition only of the lists of cloggers, clog-dancers and clog-wearing dancers, after coming to the conclusion that there are today many people, both young and old, who want to learn about clogs. There is a correction to be made to the original book - my comment that there had been only one clogger who became a Mayor. This year, Rick Rybicki has become Mayor of Todmorden. I hope his clogs show beneath his robes. Also I've learned that Jim Nelson, whose family have been clogging in Settle since 1847 also sent some clogging knives to Africa for the benefit of lepers' feet.

I have put plenty of effort into preparing the lists of cloggers and dancers, but I'm aware there are probably mistakes and omissions. In the compiling of these lists my thanks are owed to many people, but I specially want to thank Bill and Yvonne Turton, Geoff Hughes, Roy Smith and Chris Metherell. I want to thank also those people who have kept - and are still keeping - the pleasure of clogs alive. I thank too Brian Ormerod (another Accrington lad) and Barbara Blundell for their artistic contributions.

All the people I've mentioned share with me the belief that clogs have souls as well as soles.

In the past few months, I have had a lot of contact with clog-wearing dancers, and believe that their enthusiasm will keep clogs in use for many years. There seems to be more enthusiasm for clogs amongst dancers than there was twelve years ago. Two other pleasing things have happened to me lately - firstly Mitchell's Brewery of Lancaster have brought out a new ale called *"Owd Clog"* and have decided to use Brian Ormerod's drawing of a mouse peeping from a clog as their logo for that excellent product. Secondly, I learned that a Lancaster-based dance group have called themselves *"The Double-Legged Roundhouse Backsliders"* (*"The Backsliders"* for short) after coming across the phrase in a poem by my friend Alan Bond, who died recently. Alan's brother, Les, shares with me some pleasure in that. It occurs in the poem. *"The Clog Feyter"*.

Bob Dobson
Spring 1993

1.   Fundamentals

LET'S get something right before we start — what are we talking about? We're talking about the 'modern' clog — that is the footwear formed of a wooden sole and a leather upper. This basic definition will be seen to be important when we later talk about the clogs of bygone eras which could not be so described.

We will be hearing, perhaps for the first time, terms which are so closely connected with clog history as to be necessarily mentioned. The first of these terms is *patten*. When I first saw the word I thought an 'r' had been left out before the final letter. Not so. The patten, the S.O.E.D. tells us, is 'a name applied at various periods to various kinds of foot-gear, e.g. wooden shoes or clogs'. Now the only sense is a kind of overshoe to raise the ordinary shoes out of the mud or wet, consisting of an iron oval ring or the like, by which the wearer is raised an inch or two from the ground.

While we're on with definitions, let's look at the word *'clog'* and remember that it is both noun and verb. It seems to have started life as a verb in Middle English times (1150 to 1450). In the S.O.E.D. it has six meanings as a noun, including 'a wooden soled shoe or overshoe worn to protect the feet from wet or dirt'. There are seven meanings to the word as a verb, from which I suggest that the word came into use (say) about 1300 through the footwear being cumbersome and wooden. In Cumberland dialect a clog is any block of wood. Those same Cumbrians have a lovely name for clogs — 'timmer (timber) beuts'.

At this early stage I must draw your attention to the similarity between our 'clog' and the French 'sabot'. One of the earliest things I was told by historians was that our Lancashire clogs came from France and the English word was merely a translation of the French. Neither point is true. More of that later when we discuss the question of Flemish interest and a very basic difference between the two.

A matter akin to Anglo-French definitions is the translation of the Germanic word for shoes *schoen* into an English word *shoon*. This word has gone out of common use (indeed, I thought for a long time it was a dialect word only) but illustrates the way in which foreign words enter our language. In 'The Cobbler's Song' Peter Dawson sings of 'Working all day at slippers and shoon, working all day from morning to noon'. 'Les Souliers' is French for shoes. Couldn't soles come from that? The North Sea and the English Channel aren't very wide are they?

Still on this point of the similarity between words, we recall that people say of a clog wearer that he 'clomped about', meaning he made a lot of noise walking about. *Klomp* is a Germanic term for a wooden shoe, and the first reference to a klomp is about a race in 1459 to the Tower of Marienkap. I like the word. It is onomatopoeic, just as is 'clattering'.

There is one point of vital importance to be understood before we carry on. A *sabot* and a *klomp* and a *galoche* (here we are again — similar to galoshas) are dissimilar to our clog in that they are made from one piece of wood, hollowed out and not joined to leather. In reading the various authorities on footwear and fashion history, I have been struck by the way in which the meaning of 'clog' has changed slightly over the centuries. A definition of one era was not matched exactly in another.

Another term we meet is *choppino* or *cropines* or *chopines* (for the Italian *croppini*) which were high clogs worn outside the shoe in the 17th century. They were of Eastern origin.

Oakes & Hill endeavour to group all the terms we have discussed: 'The galoche, patten, clog or choppino are all forms of a wooden sole or wooden "step-in" shoe, with or without leather thongs, straps or toe caps'. They further discuss the galoche mentioned in a reference to the galoche of 1611 when it was defined as 'a wooden shoe or patten made all of one piece, without lachet of leather and worn by the poor in winter', and comment that this was probably the early English version of the sabot.

2. Wood, Leather and Clog Making

WE already know that our clog is simply a wooden sole below a leather upper (whilst a sabot is a single piece of hollowed-out wood), but let's examine how the two came to be joined, and how in fact a tree and an animal's skin became footwear fit for a king.

Firstly, I don't propose to discuss at length the process of leather making. Suffice it to say that craftsmen have been making leather for footwear for centuries and that I for one firmly believe that there is no substitute for leather — unless it's wood. There are, as we shall see, various grades or types of leather, but for present purposes let's accept leather as being a natural commodity for cloggers to use.

Now for that tree. Ideally it is an alder, although to a lesser degree birch, sycamore and willow have been used. The clog sole made by machine should be English birch, but for the craftsman it should be alder. (Oh that there were the craftsmen to use it now). The alder grows in wet places such as on river banks where it lives off the water in the ground (in fact alder seed will only germinate easily on damp mud). It is chosen because it is easily worked and absorbs moisture when in sole form. Both are very important points. It grows mostly in the wet conditions which prevail in Ireland and Wales and that is where the whole process begins.

Remember that we are talking about the days of yesteryear, probably between 1840 and 1940, and ideally about 1910 when the craftsman clogger was busiest.

A small gang of *bodgers* (itinerant woodland craftsmen) come to the chosen copse. We call them block makers. They have agreed to a price to cut down and prepare the alder ready for the use by the clogger in town. They may work for the merchant who has bought the alder, or be employed on a casual basis. On the job their shelter is the trees and a tent, though probably they will be in lodgings in some nearby township. It is a rough, healthy life they live. Good food and plenty of it is essential. It was reckoned by bodgers in Wales that the amount made from selling waste material for firewood and pea-sticks should be enough to buy all the food that the gang would need whilst working in the woods. It has been said that gypsies monopolised the bodger trade. They had a habit of leaving bark on to show that the cutter had not wasted wood by cutting the block smaller than was necessary. A difficulty encountered by those men wanting to organise trade unity was that block cutters often required other means of livelihood, particularly in winter.

Ferguson (Fergie) Kenyon of Abbeystead, Lancaster, worked in Ireland for six years, coming home in 1927 to work nearer home in the trade of block cutting. He was taught by his father to swing an axe with his feet spread apart, using two hands, and to use the cross cut saw. His father was so good that Lord Sephton brought visitors to watch his prowess.

The chosen tree is probably 50 to 60 feet high, though it could grow to 90 feet. The best wood for our purpose is near the bottom of the tree as it is free from shoots. When felled, it has to be cut first into boules, their length being determined by the knots in the tree. This boule is then to be cut lengthwise into basic blocks. The length is still determined by the knots and the blockmaker is gauging by the eye or a size stick — itself a piece of alder 18 inches long with notches at suitable distances along for the various type/sizes to cut into blocks roughly 13 inches long (for men's soles), 11 inches (for women's), 8 inches (for lads) and 5 inches (for children). His axe was put on the boule and struck with a wooden *mel* (mallet). A combination of saw, axe, mel and *beetle* (wedge) will cleave or rive the boule to the lengths. They have the advantage of always splitting the timber with the grain, whereas if the boule were rip sawn in the direction of the grain it would not be possible to avoid cutting the longitudinal fibres, thus weakening the wood. This part of the process was called *breaking up*.

We now have a cut length, the block, and the next step is to prepare it into a rough shape faintly resembling a sole. This was done mostly in the woodland by forming each one with a clogger's *stock knife* (also called a *bench knife* or *paring knife* by the bodger) before stacking them to dry, in pyramid form. The knife had a blade about 13 inches long and 4 inches wide.

Air can circulate all round them and thus drying is natural. In the modern clog factory, this stacking principle is still used. The stack would be about 8 feet high and 6 feet in diameter. A man could climb up the sides to add further blocks to the stack. The stacks had to remain in position for about nine months to allow for proper seasoning. Alder was harvested only in spring and summer. Timber from the woodland may have been dragged to a nearby timberyard if available, using chains, horses and sweat, but traditionally the blocks were collected and taken to canal wharf, railway station or Irish Sea ferry for transporting to the clogger. It was arranged through a clogsole factor or wholesaler.

Ideally, clogs are born as twin soles, paired together from the moment the block cutter shapes them. Thus equal shrinkage can be assured and the grain will fall symmetrically on either side of the cut.

The block now having arrived at the clog shop, it must now be further processed before reaching the wearer. The main tool used from now is the *clogger's knife*, also called a *stock knife* or (uncommonly) a *lath*. To describe this knife in words is a feat in itself. It is made entirely of steel, fastened to a pivot, an eye hook in a wooden knee-high bench. The knife is virtually all blade, with a shaped handle altogether 2 feet long. There are three interchangeable knives used, each similar in shape except for a different blade. To use the knife on the block, the clogger simply swings the blade downward, using the hook as a fulcrum, holding the block with one hand, operating the knife with the other, and steadying the bench with his foot or knee. The sound heard would be the steel rushing through the sappy wood. This part of clogging is an art in itself, calling for special skills which come only with practice. Some men in larger clog shops did nothing but this job. They were known as *clog sole cutters;* separate from the *seatsman* who sat down to the job and did the whole operation.

Those blades were used in turn in the process of preparing the sole for the upper. First — the *stock knife*. Razor sharp, tempered steel which had to be sharpened with a whetstone by the clogger if he wished to keep it in perfect order. Those sole makers on piece work rates made sure their blades were in trim by sharpening them at lunch time. This is the most basic of the blades, used to cut away big pieces of fresh wood. Second — the *hollower*, convex and used for shaping the upper surface of the sole to match it to the foot and to its mate in the pair. A skilful clogger could hollow the sole to perfection by feeling the customer's feet before starting to cut. Third — the *gripper*, to cut away a ridge around the edge of the sole so that the upper can fit into it and nails can be driven through the leather into the ridge. The ridge or lip is called the *grip*. The gripper blade is

12

about ¾ inch wide, far less than the others. It is in effect a curved, V-shaped gouge chisel. The first cuts it makes are slow and careful, then speeded up a little as the clogger tools out the sole perimeter with the high degree of accuracy needed. When this rebate is finished it is about one-eighth of an inch deep and a quarter to three-eighths of an inch wide, the latter dependent on the thickness of the sole.

The coming of machine-made soles, with other factors, brought about the decline in the use of the clogger's knife. Basically the machine-made sole is similar to the hand-made, but there are points we ought to compare. When alder is cut across the grain, it splits, so it is not used by the machinist, English beech being preferred. Sycamore is sometimes used but it contains a kind of grit or silica which makes the cutting machines blunt four times quicker than does the beech. Sycamore gives a much lighter sole than beech, but not as light as alder, and alder has by far the best water resistance. Beech's grain is close and even. Though hard, it wears smoothly.

The machine-made sole cannot, by virtue of its manufacture, be made *bespoke* for the individual, and this fact was an important one to the clog wearer who, always having had his clogs hand-made, found himself having to buy *off the peg* when finally machine-mades did supersede hand-mades. A deformed foot could be specially catered for in hand-mades. More on sole making by machine later.

Alder's name comes from an Anglo-Saxon word *aler*, and a German one *erle*. The roots strongly attract moisture, and a number growing together will turn firm ground into a swamp, though its roots will protect a river bank from water erosion by holding the soil together. Because of this quality, alder have often been specifically planted alongside a watercourse embankment. When growing by a riverbank, it often grows several main stems or trunks, but usually only one when standing back from the riverbank. Its leaves are broad with a depression at the apex, dark green in colour (becoming brown to black in autumn) and have shallow teeth around the edge. It bears stalked side buds most of the year, and its bark is very dark greyish-brown, almost black, which becomes broken up into small squares.

In England, alder swamps are properly called *carrs*, in Wales *gwen* and in the Scottish Highlands *jearn*. Because alder trees have been so much cut, and not uprooted, they grow again as many-branched bushes. For a tree to grow again to full proportion would probably take fifty years. Charcoal made from alder was used for gunpowder, its bark was used in tanning and in producing a strong orange coloured dye. The botanical name for the alder is *Alnus glutinosa*. It is not to be confused with a small tree bearing the name alder buckthorn (*Rhamnus Frangula*).

Alder's 'softness' makes it not only easy for the bodger and clogger to cut, it 'gives' to the shape of the foot, thus providing comfort. However its most favourable quality is its ability to absorb damp, making it most suitable for people working in **wet conditions**. Almost everyone who has ever worn clogs will say how **good they** were for the feet. One of the factors causing this is the **quality of** 'breathing', 'airiness' or 'dryness' the wooden sole imparts. **Alder was cut by the** blockmaker in the spring or summer when the sap was 'high' in the tree, using axe and cross-cut saw.

The Alder leaf

In 1923 a blockmaker was able to earn 1s. 6d. (7½p) for 12 pairs of mixed sized blocks, or 1s. 2d. (6p) for 12 small size and 1s 10d. (9p) for long size. He could make 24 to 30 dozen pairs of blocks a week, working a 10 hour day. In addition he might sell the waste wood to firewood merchants or housewives and this would bring in 35s.- to 40s. (£1.75p to £2.00) a week. (See the photo of bodgers in E.H.L. Edlin's excellent book 'Woodland Crafts in Britain', 1949, p.p. 25 & 26).

It is of interest that in 1455 members of the Fellowship of the Craft of Pattenmakers of London petitioned the king to be allowed to use a timber called *aspe* (similar to poplar, hardly ever since used for clogging) for clogs and pattens. A statute of 1416 had prevented them doing so. Aspe was used for arrow-making.

I know nothing of qualities or grades of leather but the man having to work with it soon knows which he prefers to work with and which will last. There are only two words that we need be concerned with — *kip* and *split*. **Kip** is the better, and that too is graded. When I was handed my clogs by Mr. Crawshaw of Crawshawbooth he told me they were of 'best kip'. Split is leather from the belly end of a hide.

Cloggers would buy hides from the sundriesman (a commercial traveller in the trade) working for a grindery merchant, and store them in his shop. They mustn't get too dry, nor indeed too wet, though sometimes they would be dipped in water to make more pliable.

It was on a hide that the patterns made of zinc, tin or cardboard would be placed to start off the procedure of making a clog top. In many workshops patterns were handed down from one generation to another. (This factor helped towards the preservation of 'area' styles). Dressmakers work with patterns and cloth in exactly the same

14

way. When cut and stitched the upper would be put onto a *last,* which formed it into shape, and left on it for 48 hours to allow it to set to the shape. Special pincers called *nippers* were used by the clogger to help stretch the leather over the last. Lasts would be used many times before needing replacement, and were often repaired rather than be discarded. In more recent times, spring-loaded lasts were used to make the job of taking the upper off the last somewhat easier. The seatsmen called it *clicking,* a term still in use. The cut leather would be sewn with waxed hemp thread, called *tachin end,* and the sewing started off with a bristle to keep the thread stiff. Holes were punched into leather with a bradawl-like tool called simply a *pricker.* Of course, sewing machines helped mechanise the craft, but hand sewing was often preferred by the clogger. My own clogs were hand-sewn at the heel. Mr. Crawshaw, an old-fashioned clogger, called them *jockey-backs.* My first thought was that stitching there would weaken the clogs, but in fact it gives them strength.

The last item to be put on a clog is the *welt* or *welting* or *worting* or *rand,* which is a strip of leather placed between the sole and the top to make it waterproof. It acts like lead flashing on a roof. In wet trades, copper welting is used. The welting would be cut by a clogger from a single piece of hide. At the same time, he cut laces for laced clogs. This calls for sharpness of tools, a sharp eye and a steady hand. They would be cut in a circular movement rather than being taken from the edge of a hide. The welting would hide some nails, often iron ones rather than brass if costs were being considered.

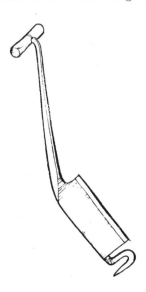

Tachin' end was not ready for immediate use straight from the reel. It had to be prepared for the bristle by being rubbed — after applying some cobbler's wax — in one direction only, on the clogger's apron. This would stiffen it, much as a needlewoman wets her thread before putting it through the needle's eye. Another useful tool at this time was the awl, which was hooked to provide a pulling action on thread, though mostly the hand was the tool used.

When the sole and the upper are both joined, they are ready to receive the *caulker,* be it iron or rubber, which helps keep the sole out of the wet and prevent wear. In many cases the *irons* have to be altered to fit a clog sole, despite standardisation of parts by manufacturers. Iron nails are used — six in front, four on the heel — and when fixed in the holes provided, the irons can be bent properly before nailing and will stay fast until ready for replacing. The bending of the irons on his *steady* by the clogger is very important to prevent the iron springing, despite the nails. A common practice was for cloggers to paint black the undersole of a new clog. This seems to have served no purpose except to make the article look good.

A Burnley film maker, Sam Hanna, has made a film of the clogger's craft, as also has the Clitheroe clogger, Richard Turner. His film is shown by Clarks, the shoe makers.

3.   Clogs through the Centuries

I WAS surprised to see the obvious ancestors of our clog in countries outside Europe and outside modern times. It would be difficult indeed to pin-point the first true clog in time or place, and I don't attempt it. We do know that the Romans wore *salepes,* a kind of wooden shoe with an affinity to the clog or galloche, and that Roman countryfolk strengthened them with nails. Perhaps it was due to Roman influence that some of the countries they occupied — Britain, Italy and Switzerland — never in fact wore sabot-style shoes.

Oakes & Hill discuss the evolution of the clog at length, mentioning the various fore-runners and referring to the use of these in a rural setting. When researching, it has become obvious to me that different writers and historians have used different terms for the same type of footwear. However, it can properly be said that pattens preceded clogs as we know them, and that galoches preceded pattens. The historian Strutt tells that wooden shoes are mentioned in the records of the 10th century in Britain, having wooden soles and uppers of some more pliant material. Pattens continued in use here until the end of the 19th century, the earliest of them being recorded in 1416. The galloche was the Gaullish shoe.

There is no shortage of eminent literary references to clogs, pattens and galoches. In 1660, Mrs. Pepys wore pattens, and three years later Marconys, a French student, visited London, saw them and described them in some detail:- 'Les femmes portent de galoches qui sont fait d'une semelle de bois assez deliée, laquelle par le moyen de deux petites courroyes de cuir s'attache sur le haut du pied et au dessous de ses semelles ou sandalles, il y a un collier de fer de quatre pouces de diametre, qui est figuré en quatre goderons de cette sorte qui a assez d'epaisseur ou hauteur pour empesher que le sandale ne touche la terre; cela fait assez grand bruit sur le pave.'

That shrewd, sharp and talented observer Defoe noted (1725) the social distinction which had arisen between clogs and pattens. The 18th-century fashionable overshoes were known as clogs and had leather soles built up underneath the instep with straps to go over the foot which were often of leather or silk to match the shoes.

17

Swift, again urging Stella to work, wrote to her in 1771: 'Use excercise and walk; spend pattens and spare potions; wear clogs and waste claret.' So it was, in the space of a few years, relatively speaking, that wooden soled shoes had become an object of fashion as well as of rural use, and, as is the whim of fashion changes, so the object moved from being 'in vogue' to being objects of scorn — scorned except by country folk. We have seen a similar occurrence in the twentieth century.

That other travelling reporter, Dr. Pococke, wrote in 1750: 'In those counties of Westmorland, Cumberland and the North part of Lancashire, they wear shoes with wooden soles, and many on working days go without stockings.' He observed the British scene in his travels and recorded them. In this reference, it is uncertain whether he meant men or men and women. A Cumbrian reference of 1777 tells of 'clogs instead of shoes the labouring people still wear, the upper part whereof is made of strong curried leather and the sole of wood shod and bound with iron'.

Published in 1788, Noel Chomes' Household Dictionary defines *Muilken*, which were pattens, as 'soles and heels of wood with a piece of Russian or other leather nailed over the top ..... used by women or girls for scrubbing and spring cleaning the house ..... made in large quantities in Gelderland, Netherlands and Germany to be exported everywhere.'

The Lancashire diarist, Rev. Peter Walkden, recorded (1729) paying 2½d. for having a pair of shoes made into clogs. His children wore them at their Forest of Bowland home. The Swedish agrarian observer, Kalm, writing of his visit to England in 1748, found pattens a novelty 'a kind of wooden shoe which stands upon a high iron ring, into these shoes they thrust their ordinary leather or stuff shoes.'

My earlier reference to the state of fashion in clogs being used by women is reinforced by Sir Frederick Eden in his 'State of the Poor' (1797). He related them to working men and gave no suggestion that they were women's wear. The Radical writer and poet, Samuel Bamford, the first Lancashire writer on the subject, mentioned the 'patten clogs' which his aunt wore about 1799 — probably these were over-clogs, not the clogs we know today. Bamford left Lincoln Prison about 1820 and gave his clogs to the friendly turnkey at the gate. He had never seen them before and thought them a curiosity. The widespread wearing of wooden-soled shoes by women in the industrial areas of Lancashire and Yorkshire seems to have been a 19th-century development.

J. Geraint Jenkins, keen observer of rural life, wrote 'the origins of this simply constructed piece of footwear are lost in the mists of antiquity, but clogs were certainly worn by rich and poor alike in the Middle Ages.' At the time of William and Mary (1689-1702) there was what Fairholt called a clog, but which was in reality a wooden shoe fastened to the sole of the shoe, leaving the heel free.

18

By 1831 the patten had returned to fashion. There were *carriage clogs* for ladies and gentlemen, made of cork or leather and worn over the shoe for its protection between door and carriage. In the period 1830-40 women wore clogs with leather tops and cork soles in muddy weather. At some early stage in the design of the clog, cork soles were introduced as an alternative to wood. How strange it is that some *fashion clogs* of the 1970s were of a similar type.

Southey (1832) refers to the differentiation between a shoe maker and the clogger's trade and uses the delightful phrase, 'clogging myself to go out into the storm', meaning putting on his stout and suitable footwear. He wore his clogs in dirty weather, but wore out only two pairs in 20 years, and re-ironed them three times before the clogs needed replacing. Thackeray must have worn clogs. He wrote of 'leaving my clogs in the passage'. Housewives of later years made their husbands take off their clogs before coming into the house, or at least enter by the back kitchen door. This rule is applied today in the house of a farmer friend.

Farmers of later mediaeval Britain are known to have worn wooden-soled leather or skin shoes, but no trace has been found of the all-wood shoe. Hollowed-out klomps or sabots are not seen in early English, French, Italian or Flemish miniatures. This was possibly because wood was so precious, being put to every kind of conceivable use. A serf or semi-freeman would not be in a position to acquire enough solid wood of the right kind to hollow out, nor would he have the money to buy from craftsmen making such goods.

To protect, unify and strengthen themselves, the London patten makers formed the Worshipful Company of Pattenmakers of the City of London, incorporated later under Royal Charter in 1670. The clog makers, that is the masters, or shop proprietors, rather than the workers, were an organised body of craftsmen as early as the 15th century. The Guild, or company, exists today. The Amalgamated Society of Master Cloggers, sadly, does not. Clog makers were an exception to the situation in which small timber-using industries had little organisation of either masters or men. The Industrial Council for Woodworking Industries unsuccessfully attempted the regulation of wages and rates, which were settled by individual firms when Fitzrandolph and Hay reported in 1926. By that date the Amalgamated Society of Master Cloggers did not include in their ranks the master block-cutters, who were for the most part itinerant woodland craftsmen. Attempts were made before World War I to organise the latter in order to prevent the undercutting of prices and the enticement of employees from one master to another by the offer of higher wages. These attempts, originated by the Master Cloggers, fell through owing to the spasmodic nature of the industry.

The grandson of Charlemagne (King Bernard of Italy, died 904 A.D.) wore clogs with red leather uppers laced together with thongs.

Many of you will by now have asked when the Flemish weavers

would be mentioned. They it was, the story goes, who actually introduced the clog to Britain about 1337. I hope that my references in the earlier paragraphs will have made you aware that clogs existed in rural Britain long before the advent of the Flemish woolworkers. Broughton gave credence to the Flemish weavers' story in his, the first serious study of clogs and pattens, and he was much quoted by later writers. A Rochdale historian, A.P. Wadsworth, spoke in 1942 to the Rochdale Literary and Scientific Society on 'The Myth of the Flemish Weavers'. He puts the blame on the author and divine Thomas Fuller for starting (in 1665) the much-copied fashion in attributing to the Dutch the introduction of clogs, jannock, linen weaving and wool-dyeing to the country. It was in 1337 that, for political (i.e. cash) reasons, Acts of Parliament were introduced imposing restrictions on foreign-made wool. A Belgian scholar, Dr. Sapher, estimated the total Flemish immigration at only 200 people and Wadsworth proves that the other industries mentioned were developed before the immigration. Thus, we must remember, the Flemish weavers did *not* introduce clogs to Britain, even though they probably came shod in them.

The making of shoes to different shapes, left and right, seems to have been common from early on, but not universal. Dr. Johnson criticised Shakespeare for saying that a character had put his slippers 'on contrary feet'.

It was the Industrial Revolution which brought clogs into their own and gave them national notice on a big scale. The mill workers needed a strong, cheap, weatherproof foot-covering and clogs were the answer. As industry increased, so too did clog wearing. By the beginning of this century, clogs were in universal use in industry throughout Britain. By the middle of the century they were almost a rarity, even in the traditional areas of clog wearing of Lancashire, Yorkshire and Cumbria.

I feel it is necessary to summarise this chapter for clarity. We know that:- (a) Clogs were different from pattens, which had a wooden sole raised well above the ground by either an iron ring or wooden cross-pieces; (b) Clogs have been in use in rural, agricultural Britain for about a thousand years in some form or another. It is not always clear just what type of footwear is referred to in old references to clogs. Similarly, they have been in fashionable use by both sexes for about 400 years in Britain, though again the term clog covers types of footwear, even overshoes, which our modern definition doesn't quite fit.

20

4.   Got Cold Feet?

ENGAGE in conversation anyone who has ever worn clogs and they will tell you, 'There's nothing better for your feet.' The same statement comes from parents of children whose tiny feet have worn clogs before progressing to shoes. They have undoubted pediatric value as formers and protectors of feet, keeping them warm in winter, cool in summer, dry and airy at all times. A combination of wood and leather that cannot be matched. Even though critics decry the machine-made sole, it does a fine job. The finished clog is a piece of craftsmanship. Consider that 'fitness for purpose' is a fundamental of design, then try to fault the clog—you can't.

From Cornwall to Caithness clogs have been worn in agricultural areas, and in certain other industries, particularly the heavy (mining, quarrying) and wet (brewing, fish preparing) ones. My earliest opinion, that clogs were worn only in Lancashire and Yorkshire in the period 1820-1940, was soon dispelled by the readers of the Daily Telegraph who wrote (over 200 of them) to tell me of wearing clogs in farms, gardens, workshops, railway works and factories and in such places as Billingsgate Market, Nottingham bleach works, Pembrokeshire farms, Cumberland village schools, Banffshire crofts, Salisbury Plain, St. Austel Gasworks and aboard Royal Navy ships. Each person except one spoke in glowing terms about their feet in clogs. That one exception, a lady, recalled as a girl she stopped wearing clogs because the leather tops cut into her ankle. She should have either rubbed them with grease to make them supple, or cut a V-shaped nick in the top edge to give the same effect. To increase the warmth in winter, many would put hay, straw or even bracken into their clogs along with their feet. Clogs usually had plenty of room in them.

And the pleasure to a child! In what present-day footwear can a child run down a street making sparks fly as the irons scrape against pavements, providing work for cloggers and headaches for parents? In what other footwear can a child collect natural stilts just by walking through snow? My schoolmates and I called them *pads*, others called them *cloggie-boggies, snow pattens, cloggins, clogballs, snowclots* and *cobs*. These stilts were removed by kicking sharply, preferably sideways-on, against a wall, pave-edge or doorstep. Few took the preventive way of pre-greasing the undersole so that snow would not stick in the first place. All this and warm feet too, though if the snow got over the tops the effect was gone.

In the wet trades, the clog soles were usually thicker than usual. Frank Walkeley's Huddersfield clog sole factory calls them *brewery soles*. The foot is thus kept that bit further out of the wet, the wood absorbs the dampness and loses it gradually when the clog is off the foot or in dry conditions. Quick drying would ruin the clog.

Still got cold feet? Take the advice of Lancashire writer Joseph Ramsbottom, who wrote in 1864, 'Doff thi clogs an warm thi feet.' (Take them off!)

The shape of the sole where it meets the foot is of the utmost importance. The hand-made sole could be 'bespoke' for an individual and was done by the clogger feeling his customer's foot, realising its contours and then transferring them to the sole by combination of eye and arm. Such a pair were the ultimate in comfort. The hand-made yet not individually-tailored sole would not be quite so comfortable, and the machine-made sole less so.

Some sole-cutters had their own ideas on what shape a sole should be. A Nelson firm, Nutter's, made a sole of most unusual design,

with an accentuated instep. The Nutters were known eccentrics, the three sons staying single and being taught to clog by their mother. Despite the steepness of the instep, customers thought highly of them and it was said. 'Once you've worn a Nutter sole, you'll never wear no other.' Perhaps the 'Nutter lumps', as they were called, were made to ensure continued custom, as the buyer couldn't wear any other by the time his feet had acquired an unnatural shape. The Nutter workshop in Leeds Road, was 'knee-deep in wood chips'. They finished trading in the 1960s. One man's sole-cutting work could often be identified as his own, as each one's style varied according to his use of the stock knife. Similarly, each clogger putting his artistic skill into finishing off a pair of *dandy, fandy* or *cooartin'* clogs would use his own designs by which he could be easily identified.

A master clogger told me: 'The more instep in a clog, the better. Machined flat soles killed the clog trade not only by numbers but also by the quality of the product — folk couldn't wear them.' Chiropodists encourage clog wearing as, due to the sole shape, muscles and ligaments are exercised, giving a strengthening effect to weak structures. Besides that, corns don't grow on clog-soled feet. Accrington people remember the town's Medical Officer of Health, Dr. Greenhalgh, wearing clogs to go about his work in the town.

In 1962 a doctor in the south of England visited Burnley at the suggestion of a colleague, Grace Ingham, doing leprosy work in Africa. He sought someone who could make a clog sole from the block. A newspaper appeal reached Richard Turner, son of a clogger and himself a seatsman who had taken into shoe repairing such skill as to be voted 'Britain's Champion Shoe Repairer' in 1951 and 1961. As a result of their discussion, Mr. Turner went to the Oji River Leper Colony on the River Niger, Biafra, in January 1963 and for six weeks gave basic training with his stock knives to the lepers, using the plentiful local wood. A type of wood-soled sandal was made to replace the rubber-tyre shoes the lepers wore.

Those native African patients needed something to support their injured feet. Dick gave them lessons in his own time and at his own expense, teaching them to shape wood and fasten uppers to them. Bisana and zigba replaced alder and beech. I have since been in touch with Dr. Felton Ross of the All-Africa Leprosy and Rehabilitation Training Centre at Addis Ababa, who praises Dick's work. He told me that, due to the acute difficulties of foot disorders, a sandal type of clog, very similar to the modern Scholl's sandal, is preferred and is very helpful in healing foot ulcers.

Mr. Turner, later to become the last Mayor of Clitheroe (1972-74), paid for the trip himself and made a film of what he saw. When shown locally on his return, it made £200 for LEPRA. Two years later he went to Uganda on a similar mission with his stock knives. Those knives will never wear out, though they do require sharpening. Now he employs two men on clogging for two days a week, but they (and he) now do *finishing* only, buying tops and ready made soles, then uniting them. I find a good deal of pleasure in thinking that a Lancashire man's craft has eased the lives of lepers. Dr. Ross, working with them in Biafra and Ethiopia, has reported on the pediatric value of what we may call clogs to his patients. The answer lies not in the soil but in the sole.

5.   The Clatter of Clogs

Two thing's, you'll find, browt Lancashire fame.
One were cotton, and t' cotton frame.
An' as fer t'other, well, there's nobbut one name,
An' that's — clogs.

—Harvey Kershaw, 'Clogs' (1958)

THROUGHOUT my life I have been interested in Lancashire, its
folk and its past. My grandmother wore clogs each and every day. As
a child I rebuked her for this habit, and she threatened to attend my
wedding in them. This horrified me, yet when the time did come I
pleaded with her to do just that, but she wouldn't. She often cleaned
her clogs with banana skins, which gave them polish and fed the
leather. Her clogs shone as clogs ought to shine. Can you think of a
better use for something that everyone throws away? There's
economy for you. Clog cleaning was always done at night, so that
they felt and looked good for work or school the next day. Many
schools had clog inspection before classes. Kids would polish their
clogs on the backs of their stockings.
   As we have discussed, the clog became extensively used when the
Industrial Revolution burst on the nation. The 1840s saw the advent
of many cloggers' businesses. In Lancashire the mills and cobbled
streets echoed to the sound of iron-shod clogs. One writer has called
that time of day when the streets were filled with the sound the 'iron-
shod reveille', as people were wakened from their beds by it. In
Darwen the noise was named 'The Darwen Artillery' from its
staccato, continual rhythm, as if machine guns were being fired.
Rubbers, used as a quieter alternative yet often called *rubber irons,*
didn't have quite the same effect.
   In the days before the turn of the century, all clogs would be
hand-made by craftsmen seatsmen in small shops. A seatsman is an
all-round expert. The age of mass-production by machine had not
yet arrived, though there were workshops in which men worked on
piecework making nothing but soles. The seatsman would be using
the patterns he or his father had designed, to pass on to future
generations, and tools he had made or bought through a visiting

traveller, called a sundriesman, from the few suppliers to his trade such as Watts & Co., of Sheffield (est. 1760), and James Horsefield of Bradford (est. 1867). Their catalogues are a joy to behold, their brass or steel clasps (fasteners) bearing intricate, delicate designs.

As happened in most trades, the master cloggers met to discuss their mutual benefit, and the journeyman cloggers (i.e. not the shop owners) had their own Societies. Most Lancashire towns had their own Cloggers' Societies, and a higher body representing those societies met at county and even national level. Herbert D. Cocker of Burnley was North of England Secretary of the Amalgamated Society of Master Cloggers. The body was wound up in the early 1950s. They held monthly meetings to discuss prices of materials and negotiations with the journeymen. Undercutting by a Trafalgar Street shop was considered bad in Burnley, where there were almost 60 shops in 1937. The society members 'put money in' to get a shop across the street to undercut the offender. They agreed with a firm of suppliers to supply without profit, and men from the other shops went to work at the selected shop for nothing. This elaborate arrangement was all because the offender was charging ½d per pair less than Society members for *ironing*.

The Society had been formed in 1873 at a Manchester meeting. Delegates from Lancashire and Cheshire and one Yorkshire town attended. There was a Yorkshire Association in healthy condition already. By 1875 there were strikes in the trade, and the Society placed 14 insertions in the Manchester Examiner & Times pleading that some reason and discretion be exercised on both sides for the benefit of the trade. A form of strike pay was paid to the Ashton-under-Lyne masters to alleviate their distress in the trying times. Of course, there had to be an annual picnic and some special gatherings. All this a hundred years ago.

That original Society of 1873 had a broken existence, though in effect it was a similar society held together by Mr. Cocker. From 1879 to 1894 there was no such body, though there were local ones. At the turn of the century, Alderman Thomas Broughton of Accrington was president, and other Accrington cloggers held office with him, a practice kept up when other towns held the executive. An alder leaf was the badge of the trade when they met at Belle Vue Gardens, Manchester, for their 1899 annual picnic.

The cloggers that it has been my pleasure to talk to enjoyed telling me of their proud trade, in some cases passed on to them by their fathers. Harold Foster formerly worked in Manchester. He had earned four shillings a week in 1912 as a 13 year old. The first job to learn was putting irons on. A derisory nickname he had used for someone else in the trade was 'Owd Clog Splitter', a term derived from the fact that if a sole was too dry it would split. A period of immersion in a bucket of water was the preventive rather than the cure. The usual working day was 8 a.m. to 8 p.m., with a half day on

Saturday coming after some years. When the factories 'loossed', the shop was full of people waiting for their clogs to be repaired in readiness for the next day. Friday was a busy day, when housewives had the money they lacked at the beginning of the week.

The atmosphere of the clogger's shop is remembered by many, including myself, who sat on the clogger's form in stockinged feet watching the clogger, his mouth full of nails or those small pieces of wood resembling broken matches used for filling in old holes before the nail was inserted. He worked with efficiency born of practice. One master said it took ten years to learn the whole art of sole-cutting, to become thoroughly expert and speedy. Twelve months was the minimum time in which a boy could become skilled in cutting out blocks, the most elementary part of the work, since his blunders could partially be remedied by the sole shaper. After work each day, leaving no work undone, the sweeping up was done.

Harold recalled being a member of a cordwainers' club for the shoe and clog trade at Swinton, and remembered those itinerant cloggers who helped out at the shops for a few days then left on pay-day, their first stop being at the pub.

John Livesey, retired clogger, of Blackburn recalled his first few weeks as an apprentice. He did nothing but make *tachin' end*. It is rubbed along the clogger's trouser leg until its component threads bind together as one tough thread. I tried it, forgot that the rubbing was one-way only and rubbed to-and-fro, with disastrous results. This early skill was to serve John well in later years. He showed me some tools that all cloggers used:

A circular-shaped *fudge wheel* used for crimping or fancy work.

A *crimper* or *groover* to inscribe the leather.

A *bosching iron*, which when warmed up on a gas ring helped to get the leather shaped onto the last.

A *clamp*, to help in sewing the clog's seam. The clog is held in the jaws (A) and the sewer's knees grip the clamp at (C). It is made of

A Clogger's Clamp

springy wood screwed together at (B). The tool is also used in saddlery.

A *pig foot* chisel to get nails out of irons.

The *steady*, also called an *iron foot* and a *last*, on which a clog is held for repair to the sole. As a boy, the steady always struck me as being like a goose with a long neck. Properly speaking, a last is a wooden former around which the clog or shoe is made.

Fred Cocker at Burnley, son of Herbert Cocker mentioned before, joined the family business fresh from school, yet was not allowed by his father to do *top* jobs like nailing irons on until he was 19 years old, in 1939. That conflicts with the training programme of Harold Foster.

Mr. Cocker's understanding of the economics, eccentricities and fortunes of the trade is profound. Doubtless his father's Association knowledge has been passed down to him. It was a trade dependent upon penny-wise policies. Used brass nails were weighed-in for scrap and the re-use of leather was prevalent. It was the practice for Burnley cloggers to go to Nelson or Colne, which were regarded as 'wealthy' clog-wearing areas, to buy at the *rag-shops* used but decent clogs for re-clogging after cleaning the kip. In fact, very few (5%) of the clogs sold in Burnley were all-new ones, the rest being re-mades. One day, collecting 'subs' for the Association, Fred told a clogger he was going to Colne to look at some kips on the coming Tuesday morning. Getting there, he found they had been sold to the same clogger, who had 'nipped over on t' bus'. Often, Cocker-made clogs would be seen coming into the shop for repair 40 years after being first made. These clogs had been *dandified* or smartened up by customers who had put extra brass nails in for effect. They didn't last long, as the extra holes weakened the leather.

As trade declined, Mr Cocker made a lot of small clogs as souvenirs. One of the last jobs he did before converting his shop into the sports equipment shop it now is, was to make a pair for Mrs Wilson, the then Prime Minister's wife, to wear in their garden in the Scilly Isles. He told me about the Nutter family of Nelson, and of the practice when buying a disused shop: 'Price for what you can see then make your profit out of what you can't see.' When he had finished clogging, he fitted out a York museum with his tools. Fred's brother, Albert, got a six-month delay in call-up to the Army when war came, as his father had a contract for supplying clogs to the evacuees. This essential job was a listed 'reserved occupation'.

Tom Walls, 93 years old (1973), retired at Blackpool, started work at the age of 13 in 1903 at Booth's, Rochdale Road, Manchester, then the largest clog wholesalers in Britain, employing eight people. They made soles only until 1920, when they took over a Westhoughton firm of the same name and started to make uppers also. Although exempted by his trade in the First World War, Tom did in fact take the 'King's Shilling'. He recalled that both soles in a pair were exactly the same shape (a common thing in the clog trade before machine-mades came onto the scene).

Shackleton's Antarctic expedition brought trade and publicity to Booth's. Tom remembered that, in 1912, two members of the party, a doctor and a teacher, came to the factory to buy clogs for the expedition and the photograph appearing in the paper was of Tom showing how soles were cut. At that time he was on piece work as a sole-cutter (he didn't become a seatsman) earning £2.5s. weekly, having started as an errand-boy. He was proficient by the time he was 17 years old, but didn't receive full journeyman's pay until he was 20, a year before he ought to have done. His early wage was 6s. for a week with hours 8.30 a.m. to 7.00 p.m. (1.00 p.m. on on Saturday). So adept was he that he could pick up any sole and tell which man made it, as each had his own style. Those clogs for Shackleton had an extra thick sole, using Welsh timber without blemishes of any kind. Tom took pride in doing the work with another top man, Bill Boston.

Returning to Booths after the war, he worked there until the blitz of 1940, when he was earning £1 per day for a six day week. His speed was not as good, but his skill was such that he trained disabled men who had entered the trade after the war. Out of every six of these men, only one would make the grade as a sole cutter, due to back trouble, visual defect showing in poor judgement, or simply — not fast enough.

Another set of clogs he remembered were those he made for Little Tich, a famous music hall artiste. They were clog soles inside 'joke' boots a yard long. Photographs often show him in similar shoes, for dancing purposes. The firm made dancing clogs too, with ash soles and patent or shiny kip tops. Some of the kip was bought as scrap from the motor car upholstery companies. One trick of the trade of the dancers was to bore a hole in the heel and place a couple of farthings in, covering the hole with a piece of tin, causing a rattle.

Tom worked in Ireland about 1928, from July to December, for experience in a *breaking up* gang in the woodlands. The summer months were always slack at Booths. He lived in lodgings and worked six days a week, cutting the damp soft wood with a conventional stock knife that he ground in his dinner time in order to 'get the big lumps off'. A large grindstone was kept for this purpose.

When working, Tom wore his *brat* (leather apron) strapped to his left leg. I asked him about the clogger's trick of having a bucket of water handy to soak blocks in. He disapproved of this except when they were extra tough, as the water soon blunted tools. It was a common practice though to keep blocks and soles in a cellar because of the damp, and a tub of water to dip leather in so as to render it pliable.

Even though no cloggers that I've heard of became rich, and it was said that the pre-war wages of cloggers in the south-west counties did not constitute a living wage, it was always a notable feature of the industry that it was comparatively easy for men to set up in business for themselves. Little capital was needed — the biggest benefit was that you were your own boss.

"BURLINGTON HOUSE,"

108 BURLINGTON STREET (*Opposite Territorial Barracks*),

MANCHESTER.

Established over 15 Years in Manchester.

Chas. M. Corlette,

Champion All-Round Dancer of the World,

Winner of the Championship of the World, at London, three successive years—1901-02-03,— and present holder of the Belt.

Winner of the Midland Counties Championship, 1899.

Holder of the World's Record of 211 steps (16 bars to a step) in 50 minutes.

Always abreast of the times with New Dances.

Trick Step, Sand, Coon (as worked by Eugene Stratton and G. H. Elliott.), Top-boot, Clog,

Wooden Shoe, Eccentric, and all Fancy Dances Taught.

Highly Recommended as a Teacher by the whole of the Theatrical Press, " The Era," " The Encore," " The Music Hall," " The Stage."

The Largest and Most Famous Academy in England.

DANCES FOR MUSICAL COMEDIES ARRANGED.

WARNING—'There is only one Corlette.' Mr. Chas. M. Corlette has no relatives in the Teaching Profession—Nor is he in anyway whatever related to any person or persons assuming the same or similar name.

6.   Clog Dancers

FIRSTLY, let me explain that the term *clog dancer* is not intended to cover the prancing dancers who dance Morris dances when wearing fancy garments and have clog-shod feet. I shall mention them in passing, but want to impress that a clog dancer is a nimble footed virtuoso who dances fast, intricate steps wearing clogs.

There were, indeed there still are, differences even within this narrow definition, and I hope to mention all types. The clogs of the purist dancer would be ash-soled for lightness, and without caulkers so as to give a sharper rap. They would be very low on the ankle, light in weight and as fancy as possible. The fanciness might be in the sheen of the leather, or the inscribed tooling called *crimping*. For either sex, the clogs would be lace-ups. The purist would dance alone, on some hard wood or slate slab on a stage or purpose-built pedestal, illustrated for me by a former clog dancer, Renee Williams (nee Cosgrove) of Accrington.

A Clog Dancer's Pedestal

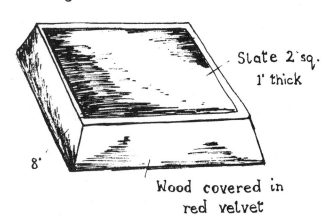

Slate 2´sq.
1´ thick

8´

Wood covered in
red velvet

Some dancers would carry such a pedestal, or a roll-up wooden mat, a board or even a flagstone from place to place. The men who carried flagstones were usually going from pub to pub to be rewarded for their pedal dexterity in liquid form.

By the not-so-purist dancer, clogs of a slightly higher style would be used. Though still below the ankle, they would be slightly heavier, without caulkers, and were really ordinary, every-day clogs kept for dancing. Only those dancers who wished to show off their talents and brighten their performance by making sparks would wear iron-shod clogs. These dancers were strictly amateurs, though often paid 'in pints or gills'. Such a one was Jimmy Lawton ('Mottram Jimmy') who as a nimble 70 year old (in 1943) carried a grey sandstone flagstone measuring 30 inches square and weighing ½ cwt from pub to pub. His strength came from his work as a builder in Ashton-under-Lyne, or perhaps from his wax moustache.

No matter what type of dancer he or she was, the steps used were the same. I don't propose to give details of them, though there aren't many. In 'The Lancashire Clog Dance' (1967) Julian Pilling records and notates some, and there is a former professional step-dancer with clog dancing experience, Sam Sherry of Galgate (near Lancaster), now teaching interested students. Thus the future of clog dancing is assured. Sam taught professional actors his art for use in a play called 'Clogs' by Stanley Wood. The play is based on John Ackworth's novel, 'Clog Shop Chronicles'.

It will now be apparent that clog-dancing was simply the forerunner of tap dancing. I quote from the 1969 'Encyclopedia Britannica':-

CLOG DANCE - a type of solo step dance performed in clogs in which the dancer marks the rythm by tapping with his toes and heels. The clogs used are of a light form of the wooden-soled-clogs once common in the industrial areas of N. England, S.W. Scotland and S. Wales. Clog dances were performed in these regions by men and girls from at least 1870, but since about 1930 they have survived only in Northumberland and Durham. Clog dancing probably originated in Lancashire, for the most widely distributed clog dances are the Lancashire and Liverpool Hornpipes. Clog dancing, after being introduced into the U.S.A. became one of the basic elements in the development of tap dancing.

Clog dancers appeared regularly on the bill of music halls, just as today's dancers appear in cabaret. Of primary importance amongst them was George Galvin, the real name of the great Dan Leno, without reference to whom no conversation on clog dancing is complete. Leno (1860-1904) was brought up on the boards as a singer and dancer, later becoming a comic. Thus, he had great ability by 1880, when Northern England was in the grip of a clog-dancing competition fever. He won a contest at the Princess Palace, Leeds, to become Clog Dancing Champion of the World. These championships were run by theatrical impressarios simply to boost box-office takings. This particular contest was a stunt by a promoter

Young Tom Walls showing his skill to visiting schoolchildren.

A conference around Tom Walls' bench.

Telephone :—HEBDEN BRIDGE, 61.
TELÉGRAMS :- MAUDE, HEBDEN BRIDGE.
ESTABLISHED 1870.

HEBDEN BRIDGE

3941
19

Bought of JOHN MAUDE & SON,

Timber Merchants and Clog Sole Manufacturers.

TERMS:-

Empty Bags to be returned before being allowed for.   Sender's name must be enclosed in each Bundle of Empties.

A bill-heading showing the advantageous position of Maude's works (courtesy of the company).

Inside Horsfield's Clog Iron Works, Bradford, probably in the 1920's, showing how mechanisation had been brought to bear on what had been a cottage industry. Horsfield's operated in Paradise Street, off Sunbridge Road, and were established in 1867. They published an illustrated catalogue showing their clasps, irons, plates and uppers (but not soles) to the clogging trade.

HENRY CARTER'S
CELEBRATED CLOGGERS' KNIVES, &c.

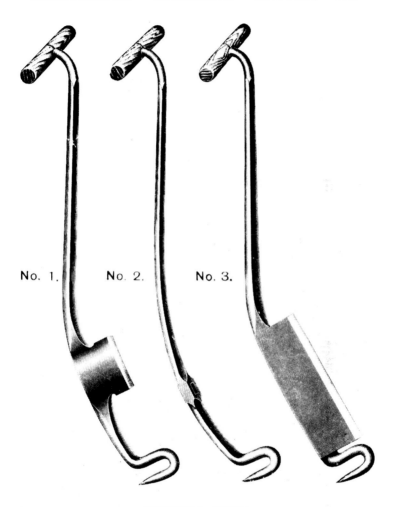

No. 1. No. 2. No. 3.

WHOLESALE AGENT:
JOHN WATTS, Lambert Works, Lambert St., **SHEFFIELD.**
Established over 150 Years.

Cloggers' knives: a catalogue illustration.

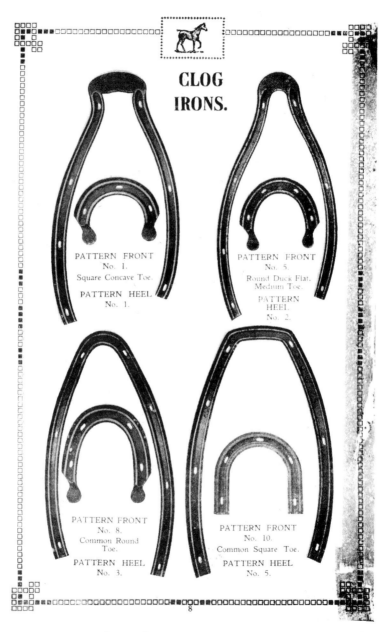

CLOG IRONS.

PATTERN FRONT
No. 1.
Square Concave Toe.

PATTERN HEEL
No. 1.

PATTERN FRONT
No. 5.
Round Duck Flat.
Medium Toe.

PATTERN
HEEL.
No. 2.

PATTERN FRONT
No. 8.
Common Round
Toe.

PATTERN HEEL
No. 3.

PATTERN FRONT
No. 10.
Common Square Toe.

PATTERN HEEL
No. 5.

og irons. from Horsfield's 1925 catalogue.

WATTS'S CELEBRATED CLASPS.

FIRST QUALITY. BRASS. FIGURED.

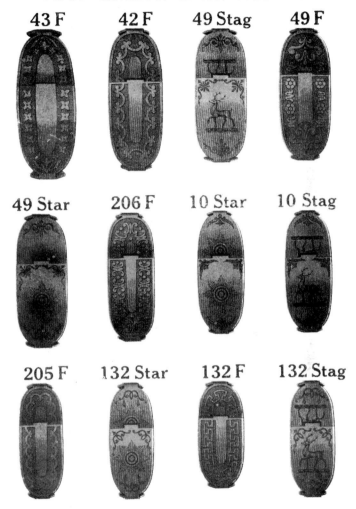

43 F   42 F   49 Stag   49 F

49 Star   206 F   10 Star   10 Stag

205 F   132 Star   132 F   132 Stag

MANUFACTURED BY

JOHN WATTS, Lambert Works, Lambert St., **SHEFFIELD.**

Established over 150 Years.

Clog clasps: a page from Watts' 1921 catalogue.

J. H. Pomfret,

Clog Iron Manufacturer,

MERCHANT IN

Clog Nails, Clasps, & Toe Plates,

And every requisite in the trade.

⊷ BACK LANE, ⊶

PRESTON.

MANLEY BROS.,

CLOG BLOCK AND BOBBIN MANUFACTURERS,

Timber Merchants, &c.,

CHEW MILL,

WHALLEY.

RICHARD RATCLIFFE,

Boot, Shoe, & Clog Manufacturer,

112, Union Road, 1, Hartley Street, & Tinker Bridge,

OSWALDTWISTLE, ACCRINGTON.

Shipping Agent for all the Principal Steamship Co's.

JAMES HORSFIELD,

Clog Iron, Clasp, and Toeplate Works,

Paradise Street, Sunbridge Road

BRADFORD, Yorkshire.

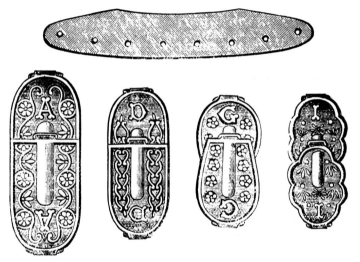

Illustrated Lists of Clasps and Toeplates on Application.

I ALWAYS have in Stock a large and varied assortment of Clog Irons suitable for any District, and can therefore supply almost any shape and quantity, without delay. My Clasps and Toe-plates are made from the very best materials, and are second to none for durability and finish. Agent for the best makes of Clog, Tip, and Brass Nails, and also for Henry Carter's Knives.

Above and opposite: Period advertisements from Alderman Broughton's 'History of the Clog & Patten Trade'.

Waitin' for th' owd Rib

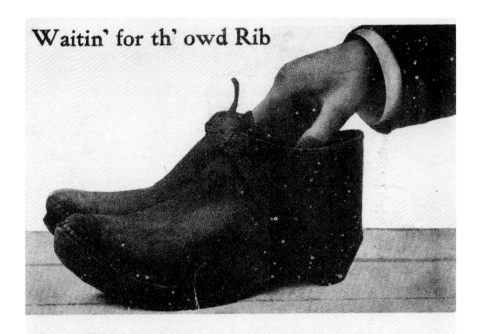

Clog post-cards of about 1900.

to bring together the leading exponents of the art, Tom Ward and Tom Robson. Encouraged by a friend to enter, Dan Leno did so and danced off with the prize, a magnificent gold and silver inscribed belt costing £50. Ward soon challenged Leno to a return match and this was held at Ohmy's Circus, Accrington (site of the Hippodrome, now gone for ever). The challenger won, but his joy must have been short lived, for soon afterwards the belt was stolen. Cashing in on public interest, yet another World Championship Contest was staged, this time in Oldham in May 1883. Dan regained the new belt, and it was inscribed for him to read:

Championship Belt won by Dan Leno
Champion Clog Dancer of the World at the
People's Music Hall, Oldham
After six nights of contests.
May 14th to 19th, 1883.

Clog dancing contests were continued throughout the North of England. Leno's father ran some in Sheffield at which Dan's belt was displayed.

Whilst most dancers were men, women are not unrecorded. Arnold Bennett in 'Clayhanger' records the greatest, perhaps only clog dance in English literature and the dancer was a woman, performing on 'a square dancing board'. There is a paragraph in the chapter on that scene that we must record: 'And thus was rendered back to the people in the charming form of beauty that which the instinct of the artist had taken from the sordid ugliness of the people. The clog, the very emblem of the servitude and the squalor of brutalised population, was changed on the light feet of their favourite, into the medium of grace.'

The other famous people whose names crop up when clog dancing is mentioned are Stan Laurel, Charlie Chaplin, Hylda Baker and Ernie Wise. The first two were, at different times, members of a troupe called 'The Eight Lancashire Lads' which was run by J.W. Jackson. In fact Jackson had a few of these troupes at the same time, performing in halls all over the country and abroad. Fred Desmond, in later years a slap-stick comic with Jack Marks, and a Blackpool Tower Circus clown, was a member of the troupes and recalls clog-dancing with them in Paris. G. J. Mellor tells of the formation, in 1896, of 'The Eight Lancashire Lads' by a Golbourne man, John Willie Jackson. Late in 1896, Chaplin joined the troupe at £1 per week and his keep. By 1906 The Lads were wearing short velvet pants with shirts and bows for dancing. Others would be more ornate, with velvet waistcoats and bright sashes.

In the competitions such as Dan Leno entered, adjudicators looked and listened for the beats, the crispness of the rap and of course carriage and originality, and often a judge would not see a performer, so as to better hear the noise of the feet. Leno used to say, 'I can only dance when I am in perfect health, for you want all your faculties awake to invent as you go on.' A Mr Coleman of Failsworth used to train a troupe of 12 lads in step dancing, and used tunes such as 'Men of Harlech', 'Auld Lang Syne' and 'British Grenadiers'.

Strange to relate, by the 1970s the art of Leno-style dancers had become part of the folk-dance scene. In 1975 at the Durham City Folk Festival, a clog-dancing workshop was held under the tutorship of 76 year old Johnson Ellwood of Chester-le-Street, son of one Jim Ellwood—both champion clog dancers. A similar workshop and a competition were held at the Fylde Folk Festival, Fleetwood, in 1977. May it be the start of a great revival.

When he was six years old, Johnson appeared on stage with his father, dancing to raise money to buy a peg leg for a collier hurt in the pit. Jim was Pitman's Clog Dancing Champion of Durham and Northumberland between 1896 and 1908. He competed again in 1924, aged 56, but failed to regain his crown. Jim had been taught by Jack Liscombe, whose daughter Ann was later to teach Fred Astaire and Gene Kelly. Another teacher of the period was George Mackintosh, who had won the All-England Clog Dancing Championship after the death of Dan Leno in 1904. Johnson was still teaching clog dancing in 1975 and estimated he had taught over 2,000 pupils.

The name of Accrington dancer Jim Cosgrove comes to the fore when clog dancing in North East Lancashire is discussed. Jim, who died aged 49 in 1934, was considered one of the world's best exponents of step dancing, though primarily a clog dancer. Just after World War I he visited the U.S.A. and Canada, returning to this country to teach step dancing, which he had probably learned in Canada whilst wearing the clogs he had taken out with him to wear to work on the railways. As a young man he is said to have come second in the World Clog Dancing Championship, and spoke of receiving help and training from Dan Leno himself. Jim had his own pedestal, made of wood six inches high with a two inch thick slate slotted in, decorated with red velvet and sequins on the side. He also had his own roll-up mat made of ash, which was very heavy. He carried this over his shoulder between appearances at different places, as well as carrying his pedestal.

Jim taught his daughter Renee the rudiments of clog dancing, though she became better known as a tap dancer. The change in public favour of tap rather than clog dancing was one element that caused this, though she admits to her inability to wear clogs, as they caught her heels. Shoes also allowed her greater movement about the stage. When practising with her father's other pupils, Renee remembers it was better to have a pianist rather than a gramophone as the gramophone arm started to jump when the dancing started. Jim had them practising for hours on end. He would tell them, 'The main thing in dancing is balance.' They practised to 'In the Mood', 'Lily of Lagoona', 'Little Dolly Daydream', amongst others. Jim's clogs now hold a flower arrangement in Renee's home in Accrington.

Another Accrington dancing teacher was Jim Parkinson, who 'could dance on a piece of glass without breaking it, and he often did so to show his skill'. He danced in lightweight, patent leather clogs, on the bottom of which resin was applied by standing in a tray containing this substance. He too had his own dancing mat. It is quite probable that tap dancing superseded clog dancing because the performers didn't have to carry a heavy mat or pedestal.

Mrs Veronica Ryan (nee Dermody) was taught by Cosgrove and Parkinson from the age of seven years, and went twice for her first pair of clogs — once to be measured, once to be fitted. She danced first (1929?) in clogs made to look like Dutch clogs and was soon to win talent competitions with Jim Parkinson in the junior and adult sections at the Accrington Hippodrome. There was no special Lancashire costume, and the performer's clogs would last for years.

By 1934 clog dancing was regarded as old-fashioned and, although a Shirley Temple film of about 1935 showed such dancing, the era of the solo clog dancer was over. Nowadays we are still fortunate enough to see Morris dancers throughout England. I'm not referring to the troupes of young girls we see at galas and festivals in summer, but to those robust, often bearded and gaily bedecked men who trip to the tune of the fiddle, flute and squeeze-box. In the North of England at least, such dancers wear clogs in preference to shoes — the fancier the better. Graham found 15 differences between 'our' Morris dancers and those further south. The seventh is, 'clogs, not shoes are the proper dancing foot-gear for the district, and boys are taught to dance in clogs, though some men wear shoes'.

It is interesting to note (but little to do with clogs) that James I, in 1681 in his 'Book of Sports', allowed people to take part in Morris dancing on Sunday so long as it didn't lead to the impeding or neglect of Divine Service. He saw that, if it was taken away from people, they would become what he called 'filthy tiplings' — drunkards. The Lancashire Hornpipe dance was famous as early as 1691, in the reign of Elizabeth I. Those dancers probably wore clogs. In the main, group dances have probably not been as keen on the intricacies of foot movement as on the body movement, punctuated by the rap of the clog. Such a group are the Britannia Coconutters of Bacup. Each Easter Saturday, this gaily-clad group of eight face-blackened dancers tour the town accompanied by the brass section of a local band and several hundred followers, whatever the weather. They dance to a total of six traditional tunes, only one of which seems to have a name — 'Clowbank' or 'The Tip Top Polka'. The others are referred to by number. I spoke with John Flynn, the group's leader, in 1974 when he was wearing a beautiful pair of clogs made for him at Rochdale in 1922.

The dress of a 'nutter' is blackened face, red and white kilt, white knee length stockings and black clogs. There have been 'nutters' since 1857. Wooden blocks called *tappers* are worn on the wrist and knees to heighten the noise, and pliable cane garlands of flowers are carried. Each man of the group is intensely proud of his participation in the traditional dance, and in his clogs. To see them dance is indeed a spectacle. It is commonly believed that the word 'Morris' is derived from 'Moorish' — as of the Moors of Morocco. Thus is is easy to see why the 'nutters' have black faces, in imitation of the 'blackies' or North African sailors. Read about the 'nutters' in 'The Bacup Miscellany' (1972 edition) by Digby and Bowden.

I ought not to close this chapter without mentionining the zany activities of some characters devised by the Lancashire cartoonist Billy Tidy — 'The Cloggies', who appear in 'an everyday saga of clog dancing folk'. They have appeared in plays too.

The Farnworth poet, Eric Holt, has written a poem which rattles off the tongue with the rhythm and rattle of clog on dancing surface:

JUMPIN' JACK

Watch 'im goo, yon gradely prancer,
Tappin' toes, an' clackin' 'eels,
Jumpin' Jack, 'ee's best clug dancer
E'er stepped eawt wi' jigs an' reels.

Twistin' turnin', peawndin', prancin',
While th' cwd fiddle sings away,
Leeter than a fither dancin'
On a breeze i' t' month o' May.

Watch yon childer clap together
Keepin' time to t' click an' clack.
Summer, Winther, onny weather,
Eawt thi cqom to Jumpin' Jack.

Carnivals corn't do wi' eawt 'im,
Churches want 'im fer t' bazaars,
O'er Sixties weren't bi beawt 'im,
Sooner 'im ner t'telly stars.

Pair on pair o' clugs 'ee's batthered,
Still 'is pins er sthraight an' thrue,
As on t' day when 'ee fust clatthered
I' new clugs when 'ee were two.

Jack lad, keep thi toes i' fettle,
Mak' eawr spirits gay an' leet,
Though thi clugs be shod wi' metal
Wi find gowd i' them two feet!

Clug = Clog in some Lancashire dialects.

7.   Clog Sports

WITHOUT question, the greatest of all sports which involves the clog is clog fighting. It must be Britain's least-recorded sport of olden times. That is possibly explained because of its tones of illegality. Basically, the sport involved (note the past tense, used in the hope that the sport is dead) two combatants kicking each other with clogs. It seems that sometimes the two were fully dressed, sometimes half-dressed, sometimes naked, and that the rules were either (a) No kicking above the knee; or (b) Kick anywhere. Holding each other by the shoulder, the loser was the first to submit. Each man kicked in turn. In 1836 a newspaper described fighting 'Lancashire style', involving kicking and throttling, being common throughout the county. The fighters would call the sport *purrin* or *parrin*, or *porrin,* which is the dialect word for kicking or *puncing.*

Convictions for manslaughter followed after these fights, and at the end of the 17th century Lancashire magistrates revived the punishment of burning in the hand for men convicted of manslaughter under these circumstances. They were organised in secrecy, as was cockfighting. There were phrases used in connection with the sport:- *up an' deawn feytin* — a fight in which both hands and feet were used; *clog-toe pie* — a jocular term for a good kicking; *arbitrators* — clogs. In the Lancashire Records Office are statements from witnesses of an organised clog fight near Bury in 1838, when the two combatants were arrested. The fight lasted half an hour and there were 200 to 300 spectators.

Arnold Bennett's classic 'Clayhanger' (1910) has a clog fighting scene — not the sporting type, but a fight born of hatred one man for the other. A similar scene is found in Thomas Armstrong's epic 'King Cotton'. To read it is to feel the pain, smell the sweat and blood as Clogger Lynch and Abel Nuttall join battle:

> Voluntary stewards, working strenuously, had at last cleared a space which would suffice but which, by acknowledgement clog-fighting regulations, was somewhat restricted.
> Jemmy Caffrey, as in that previous contest, was the master of ceremonies, and holding up his hand for silence, began to summarise the rules .... Antagonists to face each other at the start a foot apart .... arms to remain at the sides and not to be used for fending off .... chest tupping permitted .... scooping and hooking with feet not

barred .... fore and back lunging allowed, either with toe-cap, side of clog, heel, or irons .... man down could be kicked on the head or in the face if he did not admit himself beaten, and in any portion of the body except the private parts.

'An' if he's kicked there', Jemmy Caffrey said warningly, 'th' offender is held fast and th' other can have a go at the same place. That is,' he added grimly, 'if he's able to get up an' take it.'

The Manchester folk singer, Harry Boardman, has recorded a song which concerns a clog fight between two suitors in which the fight is to take place 'on th' Owdham plan — a regular up an' downer'. The song, 'Sam Shuttle and Betty Reedhook' (on 'Owdham Edge' — Topic Records 12T204) is derived from an undated broadsheet ballad.

There used to be a pub called 'The Clog Dancer' on the site of the Duke of York Hotel, Heyside, Oldham, but it was closed down after a man was kicked to death in a puncing match. There was a 'Clogger's Arms' in Bank Street, Accrington, in 1869 but it too disappeared. The likelihood is that there were others in other northern towns. There still is one at Lee Street, Uppermill, Oldham. Pairs of clogs adorn the bar and the frosted glass windows bear the name. One of the clogs in the bar was used as a model for the clog depicted in the crest of Lord Rhodes of Saddleworth, who lives nearby. He is probably the first and only titled gentleman to use the clog in his crest, it being intended to depict his working class background and affinity with Lancashire people. He was MP at Ashton-under-Lyne for many years.

Larwood & Hotten's 'History of the Signboard' tells us that the clog was often used as a shoemaker's sign in Lancashire and the Midland Counties, and also in those parts of London where that article was worn. The Lancashire County Museum Service has a fine example of a clogger's metal sign and other artefacts which it exhibits throughout the county. In Blackburn there is 'The Clog and Billycock', a name having references to the dress of local timber trade workers and a former landlord. A billycock is a type of bowler hat.

Just as nowadays people go in for setting and breaking unusual records, so did our forebears. Just over a century ago one Poplin, described as 'the champion clog walker of the world', achieved his target of 50 miles in 10 hours from the Queen's Hotel, Rawtenstall, walking to a point 2½ miles away and returning. This he did twenty times, finishing with 20 minutes in hand. *Clog-toe pie* was that punishment meted out to an opponent through the medium of the clog. 'Give him a taste o' clog pie' was the predecessor of the encouragement, 'Introduce him to Stead and Simpson', meaning 'Kick him!'

I understand that in South Lancashire clog fighting continued until about 1920 at least, though of course on a reduced scale and in strict secrecy. It seems that clogs were adapted in past times. I came across the word 'clog-edge' in a glossary of Cumberland dialect. It is defined thus:- 'By bending the ankle sufficiently to throw the weight of the body on the inside edge of the clog caulker, a boy obtains a substitute for a skate. Progress is not very rapid and the action is not graceful.' Mums and dads wouldn't like it either.

Young Albert Moss attended a Blackburn school in 1917 as a scholar transferred from another school. He was soon initiated into the school sport of *clog wrossling* (wrestling) in which the toss of a coin decided which of two combatants was to have a position sat on the school wall, 3½ feet high with an inverted 'V' coping. The boys had clogs on their hands. The 'wall' boy would then leap from the wall onto the other, battling on the floor. Albert recalled attending the Accrington Road Council School on his first day in boots (or rather a boot and a shoe, as he had a foot deformity) and getting thrashed by the other boys for his 'softness'. He pleaded with his parents who relented and ordered him some clogs. When they came, to his disappointment they were lace-up boots which had been clogged (clog soles on boot uppers). This drove him to stealing (a pair of clogs) for the first time in his life. He went in his acquired clogs and had a fight with the weakest lad in the class. He won and split the lad's head open. For this he got the cane, then adapted his style

to having one clog on a foot, the other on his hand.

The Manchester writer, the late Paul Fletcher, recalls a young lad playing some boisterous, rough lad's game called *thrust*. In this he got a cauliflower ear that lasted a lifetime by forgetting to cover his ears with his elbows and receiving a brass-capped, iron-shod clog in his ear-hole.

Clog jumping is a sport little heard of and apparently not recorded in depth. I suppose it involved high or long-jumping whilst wearing clogs, in competition with others. I was pleased to see a new sport coming to public notice in 1975 — *clog cobbin*, or clog throwing, in which each individual or team member stands with the field behind him and throws a large clog as far over his shoulder as he can. In team events, each member is allowed two *cobs*.

It is proper here to include the sport of young clog wearers. I was not aware of any term for the sport, though I have learned that *dowelling* or *scutting* covers it. This may be derived from *scooting* or *scuffing*. I would have called it *sparking*, as it involves a swinging movement of the clog-shod foot and bringing the caulker into contact with a flagstone. Watch the sparks fly! They flew even better against a tramline I'm told. Ben Brierley, the Lancashire writer, 'struck fire' in the 1830s in a Sunday School procession and got a hiding for it. I'm sure that if a researcher were to ask ten people in the street, 'which picture comes to mind when I mention the word "clogs" to you?', the answer of eight would be 'sparking'.

8.

Clogs in Daily Use throughout Britain

MY early belief that clogs were purely a Lancashire/Yorkshire commodity was, I am pleased to say, quashed beyond recognition after I appealed in the Daily Telegraph of 9th July, 1973. The 200 replies I received convinced me that people in all walks of present-day life were very proud of their days as clog wearers and confident as to the pediatric value and suitability-for-the-job of clogs. I was able to build up a picture of 19th-20th century clog wearing in Britain on an imaginary map. It showed clogs in use in a Cumberland village's school by all 42 pupils (1941); Macclesfield factory workers (1914); Cardiganshire farm workers (1920-30); Haverfordwest farmers (1924-30); Banffshire crofters (1902); Cardiff and Grimsby fish workers (1903-28); Sussex farmers (1914); Dumfriesshire farmers (1900); Cornish gas workers (1935-53); as well as telling me about clogs being used today by the fish trade workers and brewery workers throughout the country. Though I don't apologise for it, my book is Lancashire-biased, but I know that the people who wrote to me felt just as proud of their clogs as Lancashire folk, no matter where in the British Isles they lived. The clatter of clogs on pavements in the early hours as millworkers went to work is remembered by many Lancashire people. It woke them from slumber. On Gary and Vera Aspey's record 'A Taste of Hotpot' (Topic 12TS299) is a song called 'Coal hole Cavalry' about a lad in bed hearing the sound and translating it to be the sound of cavalry.

In the 1970s it became fashionable, in a small way, for young people to wear clogs of coloured leather. A similar situation arose in the early 1940s, as a result of a Deanna Durbin appearing in a film with a Lancashire background. George Travis of Ashton-under-Lyne made the clogs for her to wear in the film. When he was 13 years old he had won first prize for clog-making in an All-England competition. We know that Beatrix Potter, living near Hawkshead in the Lake District, wore clogs at her home and when walking in the village.

Sam Bamford, in his 'Passages in the Life of a Radical' (1842) provides us information on the absence of clogs in Lincolnshire about 1820. About the same time he recorded the normal working-class dress of pre-industrial revolution Lancashire, but made no mention of clogs, though we know that he wore 'shoes with patten clogs', which sound like over-clogs rather than what we know as clogs. I could write much more about Lancashire people's involvement with the clog, but I refrain. However, I can't fail to quote from Paul Fletcher's book 'The Clatter of Clogs' (Isn't that a splendid title for a book?). Writing of the local 'penny rush' at the cinema or meeting hall in the gas-lit, silent-film era, he says:

Without exception, the 2½d's were filled with kids, all of whom wore clogs. Anyone shod otherwise would have been thought either socially superior or a bit of a fairy.... Harry, a gifted pianist, was at his best when soldiers galloped to the rescue of a beleaguered garrison. In this he was accompanied by an ever-increasing clatter and roar of hundreds of children's clogs, stamping in unison on the wooden floor.

It seems certain that clogs of the type we are talking about have been used by working people for centuries, though it is difficult to say just when they were first used in England. It is noteworthy that none appear in illuminated manuscripts, so often the source of recorded knowledge of our past. Certainly by 1750 they were in habitual wear by working people in the North-West, and often worn without stockings.

Writing almost a century later (1839), J. Devlin stated:

In North-West England, there are still workmen of this (cloggers) profession (most of whom) travel from place to place.....the trade has long been on the wane. Type of footwear which is allied to the clog is the "backster", "mudboard" or "Mersea patten" worn by longshoremen e.g. on the Essex coast today. This is a wooden or cork board fastened to the boot with rope or straps, which by its flat and large area prevents him from sinking into loose sand or mud, as does the camel's splayed foot or a duck's webbed foot.

As we know, the clog is ideally suited for certain 'wet' trades (fishworkers, gardeners, brewerymen), this being on account of the insulation of the foot through wood absorbing the moisture. However, the wooden sole also insulates the foot from heat. Modern technology in industry made the design of clogs fit to cope with excessive heats and static electricity necessary. Frank Walkeley came up with the idea of insulating them with 'inside' felt liners. He devised too a spark-proof alloy caulker, as well as copper ones with countersunk screws, for use in explosive situations. He had adapted also to provide protection against fluids used in the car factories. Although boot polish would be used to advantage by outside workers intent on lengthening the life of clogs, a good many found that dubbin was both cheaper and more suitable. Women seem to have preferred polish.

As clogs were 'protective' clothing in the Second World War, and thus 'essential', companies issued them to employees without restriction. Walkeley had to obtain licences to make clogs and buy leather on his demob after the war. He now makes a thicker type of sole specially for brewery workers. In the 1939-45 War, the Government's 'War Civilian Footwear Control Order' distinguished two types of clog—(a) clogs proper for which irons were required; and (b) munition workers' clogs for which no irons were required.

The Stork Margarine factory in the Wirral employ their own clogger, though now they are worn by only about 100 workers there. It is estimated that between 1918 and 1950, there were 1,500 pairs in use there.

Evelyn Vigeon gives interesting statistics derived from the directories and census returns for the number of cloggers in employment in England and Wales and in the northern counties. (Vigeon, 'Clogs, or wooden soled shoes', 1977).

B.B.

9. Decline of the Trade

IT WOULD be wrong to blame a single factor for the decline in the wearing of clogs. If we are to date the start of the decline, then we must look about 1950. The war years had been heydays for cloggers. In her book 'Made in England' (1939) Dorothy Hartley wrote:

'Clogs are now ceasing to become a mass-production article and are becoming again the work of the smaller country maker.' She attributed this to the closure of pits. I can't help feeling she had somehow misinterpreted what she saw, though we don't know just when she made her notes.

The Hebden Bridge firm of Maude's supplied the following number of soles in the years shown, in dozens of pairs:-

1906	-	71,791	1941	-	70,483
1911	-	71,847	1943	-	100,939
1915	-	100,862	1951	-	39,099
1921	-	77,614	1961	-	13,695
1931	-	77,153	1971	-	10,050

Their prices went down between 1921 and 1935 due to the depression, but then went up gradually.

John Maude had started as a clog sole manufacturer in 1870, making domestic clogs. He went 'bust'. His son James took over the business after marrying well, and in fact paid the creditors double the amount owed. For this he received a marble clock from the Halifax Chamber of Trade. Power for his machinery was provided by a waterwheel, and his circular saw and sole-cutting machine had been bought as a single lot in an auction. His firm bought the Snaith firm of British Clog Soles about 1963 and itself was bought by Frank Walkeley of Huddersfield in 1972.

However, the arbitrary date of 1950 and the figures provided don't tell about the gradual replacement there had been of machine-made soles and tops for hand-mades. No mention either of the National Coal Board banning iron-shod clogs in the early 1950s in favour of steel toe-capped safety boots. Nor of that fickle thing, fashion, in those post-war years. Clogs had become, in some eyes, associated

53

with poverty and the working class, to be forgotten in the years of plenty. I was obliged to wear shoes at Accrington Grammar School, though I wore clogs at Junior School, changing schools in 1952. The craftsmanship factor isn't mentioned either. The number of people who could wield a stock knife and cut a leather lace from a sheet of kip diminished, and would be difficult to replace in competition with factories with welfare clubs and good working conditions.

The competition must not be overlooked. The rubber wellington was being produced by the million, as was leather and synthetic footwear. Despite qualities which we recognise, clogs could not compete with these other products. There had been an effort at 'selling' clogs in the 1920s and '30s by the establishment of a Clog Publicity Association, which was a union of companies and organisations centred on Maude's office at Hebden Bridge. Sam Morgan was the secretary and only employee. He was company secretary for Maude's, and his son Maurice, who followed him into that latter job, still gets letters addressed to the Clog Publicity Association.

By the 1970s the number of clog shops had been drastically reduced. Even those remaining cloggers were not, in the main, able to fashion clogs from anything but factory-mades. I count myself lucky to have had a beautiful pair of clogs hand-made in 1973 by Mr. Crawshaw of Waterfoot at a cost of £5 5s. Despite new and faster machinery, the clog factories had to face manufacturing difficulties. Costs increased tremendously. English timber became virtually impossible to buy. Improvisations had to be devised, and secondhand leathers used. Frank Walkeley altered a machine designed to make golf club heads and replaced rubber soles with neolite ones.

A 1926 report said that 'trade competition is felt severely, but it is as yet uncertain whether the machine-made sole can entirely replace the hand-made, which is at present so much more comfortable. The abnormal demand for clogs in the (First World) War, when infants ceased and the number of industrial workers increased, stimulated the development of clog factories, until the higher wages of the industrial workers made boots more accessible to them. The wearing of clogs is felt by the industrial worker to stamp him a class inferior to that of the wearer of leather soles.' In 1922 a block cutter who visited half a dozen Yorkshire industrial towns could not obtain a single order for blocks. This was partly due to the competition of the cheaper factory-made clogs, partly to the general trade depression, and partly to the decline in the use of clogs.

I found Mr. Cocker at Burnley a sage who had considered in depth the decline of the clog trade, especially as regards the individual clogger. He remembered wisely that very few cloggers were good businessmen too, and drew the interesting parallel between the Lancashire spinners rejecting Hargreaves' 'spinning jenny' and the Lancashire cloggers' fighting machine-mades. They didn't want to accept change.

I have carried out a survey in Preston using various directories to help plot the ups and downs of the clog trade, though assuming a constant population which is probably inconsistent. In 1824 there were eleven clog and eight patten makers (some were shown only as patten makers, but by 1882 this term had disappeared). In 1854 there were 35, increasing to 47 in 1869, to 73 in 1882 but decreasing from then on to 71 (1901), 63 (1922), 51 (1932), 31 (1936) and to 16 in 1948. By 1960 there were none. In 1922 there were four clog iron makers and four clog block makers. In 1968 there was one 'clog stockist'. In each year shown, several cloggers have more than one shop. In the 1824 Baines 'Directory of Lancashire' there are many cloggers shown. Only one was a woman — Alice Marsh at Leigh. I bet she was a character.

If right is right, clogs will live for ever. They have souls as well as soles.

10   Clog Sayings

CLOGS have crept into idiomatic speech since becoming
Anglicised. Here are a few examples:-
From clogs to clogs in three generations. There have been countless
plays and films in which the theme of the story is that a local boy
(clog wearer) makes good, passes business on to his son, who by this
time was 'posh' (shoe wearer), and he in turn passes it on to his
wastrel son who ruins the business and is reduced to poor circumstances, necessitating the wearing of clogs.
A face you could clog. This was said of a person who had a hard,
craggy, unsmiling face.
   Some clogs were made with square toes. They were preferred when
a job called for a lot of kneeling, but of course they lead to the saying
that *they allowed a chap to stand closer to the bar.* I tell elsewhere
about clogs sounding on the footpaths of industrial towns in the early
morning. It has been called *clog music* and undoubtedly would be
music to the ears of employers.
   Someone who had been ill but who was expected to get better to
work again would be told, *you'll clog again.* It was used too of
persons recently having lost their spouse. *A real clogger* has nothing
to do with craftsmanship, but is said of a footballer who kicks clums-
ily and heftily or kicks his opponents. *To clog* somebody means to
kick or threaten to kick someone. Anyone who makes too much noise
would be told, *Tek thi clogs off.* It would be said of a habitual beer
drinker that he *would supale out of a sweaty* (or old pit) *clog.* I have
heard it said, but doubt its truth, that the wearing of clogs in child-
hood did not enable the muscles at the back of the leg to develop.
Make your own judgement on that. A Yorkshire folk-saying is that
*thunder means that someone is telling lies and has gone to heaven
with clogs on.*
   Pattens come into folk-sayings too. One which is certainly 16th
century at least is:-
   Had ye heard her, how she began to scolde
   The tongue it were on pattens, by him that Judas solde.
Roughly translated, this means: 'By Christ, if you could have heard
her, how she could natter and go on.'
   The French used the sabot in colloquial expressions: *Chanter*

56

comme un sabot (to sing like a clog—badly); and *On dit qu'ils melent leurs sabots* (people say they are living together unmarried). The words saboteur and sabotage have the same source (sabot), but have little to do with wearing of clogs, though I suppose if a clog wearer kicked something hard enough the object would break or be damaged. Sabotage didn't occur as an English word until 1910. I have been told that its early French meaning was to kick to death or to injure severely by kicking.

A rural member of a Lancashire Women's Institute recorded the saying, *It's clogs and cowd watter this morning,* which means, I suppose, that each day was started without luxuries such as hot water and shoes. Another Lancashire saying is, *Wait for shoon till clogs winna come.* When said of a young lady it means that she is 'on the shelf', having waited for a partner matching up to her high ideals until she is no longer a suitable catch herself. Aren't people cruel? A saying recorded in Cheshire in 1670 is, *I'll make one, said Kirkham, as he danced in his clogs.* It refers to any officious person who persists in enterprises whether properly equipped or not.

11.   Clog-Shop Memories

ONE of the great pleasures for all generations, now regrettably passed, was the time spent in a clogger's shop, waiting for the clogger to finish work on your clogs. There seems to have been a uniformity of design about these shops. They were invariably ill-lit, with the dust of years everywhere, as was the aroma of real leather. Entering the shop, one saw a wooden bench, *the form,* for customers to slide along whilst waiting their turn towards the head of the queue. On it sat old men smoking pipes, women with babies, and a hoard of kids. Most would be in stockinged feet, as the clogger had their only pair with him on the opposite side of a huge (for me as a lad anyway) wooden counter fastened to which was a brass foot-gauge, similar to a ruler.

The clogger sat there, working for all to see, on a stool that belonged to Methuselah's clogger, hammering away at clog soles that had been mended a score of times before. He sang and joked with the kids, and yarned with the men. But how? — for his mouth was full of nails, which he nimbly extracted when the need arose. He was surrounded by the tools of his trade. In the far corner his bench and stock knife, with the spare blades hung up on the wall, and near to him a tray containing all he would require — nails, bits of wood like broken matches, and *tachin' end* (a waxed gut thread). On a rack above him were the fittings for clogs — irons and rubbers of all sizes from baby's to giant's. In a drawer of the counter were other fittings such as clasps, buttons and toe-plates. The floor was covered in wood shavings, and on the shelves were clogs awaiting his attention. On the windows and walls, and hung from any convenient place were notices and adverts. Of course they were dusty and hardly legible. They hadn't been changed for ages, except to replace one price list with another, or amend the existing one. A notice of this kind hung in Richard Turner's Clitheroe shop, showing that 1939 prices were cheaper in fact than those in the 1920s. I can't imagine that situation will ever arise again.

In 1974, I went to a clog shop in Baxenden, near Accrington. Inside I found Jack Walmesley repairing shoes and clogs. On the dust-covered wall was a 1941 calendar, and a slate. In the corner was his *steady* with its goose-neck-shaped top, and its base worn away by the constant gripping of his and his father's feet. Jack told me he

TH' OWD COBBLER

Th' owd cobbler's well liked bi his nayburs,
He patches an' mends o ther shoon;
He sings th' long day throo o'er his labours,
Ah' allus to some merry tune.
No matter whenever yo' see him,
He's at it fro' mornin' to neet;
It fair does one good to be wi' him,
For his nature's so sunny an' breet.

He luvs to "rive eawt", as he co's it,
For melody flows in his veins;
Content fills his heart, an' he shows it
Bi th' gladness 'at rings throo his strains.
"This world's nooan so bad as folks reckon",
Aw've mony a time yerd him say;
"An' yo know not when Deeath's hond may beckon,
Sooa try to mek th' best o' yor stay".

He ne'er looks ahead to seech sorrow,
For he larnt, long ere reychin' his prime,
'At most joy fro' life we con borrow
Bi livin' one day at a time.
Wi' him, as wi' th' rest o' poor mortals,
Things neaw an' then gooa a bit wrong;
But when trubble enters his portals
He chases it eawt wi' a song.

Th' owd cobbler's as blithe as a cricket -
No minit i' th' day he finds dull,
An' till th' Scythe-bearer bowls deawn his wicket,
He'll enjoy life's innings to th' full.
He cares nowt for fame's empty bubble,
No riches hes he to tek wings;
But a mon 'at con sing away trubble
Is one to be envied bi kings.

had enough clog trade to keep him in a living but it would be foolish to neglect his shoe-wearing customers. In his cellar he found me a block left over from the days when he and his father cut their own soles. He recalled the balmy days of 1920 when a good sole cutter could earn £2 a week, and the times when Accrington Co-op Society had eight or nine clog shops with two or three men in each. Jack's father was a deaf mute, loved by all and known as 'Jacky Dummy'. The shop still gets called 'Jacky Dummy's' by locals. Quite likely he was put to clogging as a job he could do without the need to speak, and at which he could excel. The slate was used by him to convey messages, though it was used too by children doing their sums in the shop to while away the waiting time.

The Lancashire writer John Askworth (a pen-name he preferred to his own — Fred Smith) realised the value to the village of the clog shop, its tenant and the callers. He built round them in his books, 'Clog Shop Chronicles' and 'Beckside Lights'. A Methodist minister in Pennine circuits, he was drawing from life when he wrote the stories.

A delightful poem is one by William Baron of Rochdale (1865-1927), reproduced on page 59.

We have discussed the advantages of clogs over shoes, and these merits are well known. None knew better than grandparents and parents, who ensured that each new child, when old enough, got a pair of tiny clogs to help it learn to walk and tread properly through life's early stages. Many of you will be able to recall or even produce the clogs made for you and treasured through later years as a memento. As I write, I have suggested to my younger daughter that she passes on her first clogs to our new baby. The merits of clogs are well known by all old folk. My grandmother wore clogs to her dying day and praised them to one and all. The occasion was 'posh' if she wore shoes.

Jimmy Fell, of Whalley wrote the poem opposite. I have read it to many people, and have been told many times how very true it is.

Gracie Fields, a Lancashire lass if ever there was one, and responsible for the southerner's belief in northern caps, clogs and shawls, remembers a customer in her grandmother's chip shop: 'Sarah had her own nickname for everybody. She would call out, "Sloppy Clogs — Twopence". This was a woman who always shuffled her way into the shop in clogs a size too big. She owed 2d on the slate.' 'Our Gracie' will always be remembered by her signature tune 'Sally', the lass who dressed in clogs and shawl

A South Lancashire dialect pronunciation of ˆlogger is 'clugger', and Louisa Bearman uses it in her reminiscent poem 'Clugger's Shop' which you can read in her book 'Poems in the Lancashire Dialect' (Dalesman, 1977), or hear on her record of the same name (Big Ben BB00.06). Good stuff!

60

T'RING O' CLOGS

What ses Lancasheer to thee?
Is it Blackpoo' by the sea?
Is it wet ond muggy days,
Ships on't Mersey through the 'aze,
Blackpuddings on a plate in't shops,
Industry as niver stops,
Is it shawls or whippet dogs,
Or is it just the ring o' clogs.

Tha maybe thinks o' Pendle 'ill,
Or weivers torning out fray t'mill,
'Appen t'Rovers or North End,
Weekend when tha's brass to spend.
It's 'appen t'pits ond slag 'eaps grey,
Shrimps ond Southport, Morecambe Bay,
Or gorse, ond milistone grit ond bogs,
It brings 'em back does t'ring o' clogs!

Th'owd windmill tall on Lytham Green,
Fact'ries and th'ouses in between,
Clanging trams ond cobbled streets,
T'Market lit wi' flares at neets,
Gracie when hoo's singing "Salley",
Rivington, or t'Ribble Valley,
Mill lodges thick wi' newts ond frogs,
Mem'ries flood back wi't ring o' clogs!

Brass bands on Sunda' into t'park,
Cooartin' in t'lamp leet efter dark,
Treats on Knucknowles, Whit processions,
"Lakin", "Wichert", owd expressions,
These mem'ries rise up sharp ond clear,
When the sound o'clogs Ah 'ear,
It sweeps away the mist and fogs
Fray memory, does t'ring o' clogs!

61

12.   Machine-Mades

WE MUST remember that there are basically two parts of a clog —
sole and upper. Both were initially made by hand, to be superseded
by machine-made ones. Most working cloggers of relatively more
recent years did not mind so much the machine-made upper, but
strongly resented the advent of the mass-produced sole. The first
patent for a wooden sole-making machine was taken out in 1818 by a
Derbyshire turner, to be followed by others. Even by the turn of the
century, however, very little machinery had been introduced into the
trade, although a firm at Bootle had been quite successful in making
soles by machine. The machine-made sole didn't make much
impression on the trade until about 1921.

I had the advantage of a visit to an *upper* and a *sole* factory, both
owned by Frank Walkeley. The former is at Huddersfield, where
waxed hides, known technically as butt splits, are bought from the
leather merchant. *Best kips* have not been used for over 20 years, due
to the high price. Other types of leather are employed for clogs
intended for use in special trades, and some second-hand leathers are
used. Economy is a constant consideration. Additionally, felt (for
clog linings, providing comfort and warmth), rubber and synthetic
materials are purchased for special orders. Foundry regulations
provide for the use of only certain standards of leather for footwear.

The large hide is cut by an operator using a *clicker,* a tool so called
from the noise it makes and one which is used throughout the footwear trade, and shaped using patterns just like those of the
traditional clogger. From then on the work is done on machinery —
sewing and skiving machines. The process, up to the finished upper
being hammered onto a sole by a clogger using traditional pincers
and brass nails, is not over-mechanised. It merely speeds up what the
seatsman formerly did. Due to his intense involvement with the
trade, Mr. Walkeley has been able to introduce new innovations that
the seatsman would not have been able to do.

The sole factory at Hebden Bridge is a four-storey mill a hundred
years old, built alongside a river and a road. Beech wood arrives here
to be first cut into the required dimensions and then stored inside to
allow for seasoning. When ready for use, it is planed and cut into
blocks which are stacked to allow air to flow round them, just as the

bodgers did years before in the woodlands. The quality of wood is of the utmost importance. Just before I arrived, Mr. Walkeley had been forced to turn down a £100,000 Norwegian order because he could not buy the proper timber. Sycamore, though much lighter than beech, contains more silica, and blunts the machines four times quicker.

The main machine to be used in turning the block into a sole is now totally automatic except for the loading and unloading. Improved recently, and adapted from a machine to make golf club heads, it cuts through four blocks simultaneously to produce two rights and two lefts. The template that the machine uses as a model is of cast iron, probably from a hand-made or hand-improved sole by one of the long-serving staff still competent with the stock knife.

From the cutter, the soles are placed in a huge tumble-drum with an amount of wax and spun for three hours until they are smoothly finished. In the space of a working day hundreds of soles can be fashioned from blocks, a considerable speed-up on the traditional way. However, as we discussed elsewhere, the individual wearer's requirements are not taken into account, and factories such as the Hebden Bridge one had a tremendous effect on the lives of cloggers and wearers when factory-mades were introduced onto the market on a large scale.

Frank Walkeley recalled that the decline in demand for clogs started about 1950, after a heyday about 1946. It didn't help the trade when the National Coal Board banned clogs from mines for safety reasons. To combat this, he made clogs with reinforced steel toecaps. Even in factory-mades, there are varieties of style in both sole and upper. When Mr Walkeley took over, Maude's made 27 different styles of sole, now reduced to about ten. Areas prefer styles long established there. Gone now are *ducktoes* which are longer in shape than *commons* and *squares* (also known as *London's* because London customers like them).

So far as uppers are concerned, I have been bombarded by people telling me, for instance, that Cumberland clogs are different to Lancashire ones. This is true to some extent but it must be realised that, even in one county, there are different styles. Working clogs for farmers, often called *muck clogs* or *country clogs*, would be different from a *low clog* for a mill worker. The styles grew from people preferring clogs which they had always worn, and cloggers using patterns popular with customers. Strange that females rarely wore *lace-ups*, and that men never wore button-fastened. Both sexes wore clasp-fastened, which were favoured by miners, because they were quickly released in the event of a foot being trapped.

Though not associated with factory-mades, the matter of style brings me to mention those clogs known in Lancashire as *cooartin clogs, dandy clogs, fancy clogs and Sundi clogs* — those kept for best. Ankle high, they would be full of brass nails and of highly-polished

63

leather with fancy patterns cut in. Brass eyelets were often employed to give extra class and pattern, and sometimes a leather tab over the laceholes. Tabs were also to prevent wear on the eyelets. These fancy clogs figure strongly in the memories of working people who had little else in which to show off or take pride.

I don't want to move away from factories without discussing the clog iron, the *caulker* or *coker*. Fate allowed me to visit the last clog-iron factory in Britain on the very last day it was open. Messrs. Buck and Abbot of Preston had finished production two weeks previously, but June 8th, 1973, was the close-down day. I found Jack Buck burning rubbish and dealing with a scrap metal buyer. I was saddened to see a bit of industrial history passing to the scrap heap, but Jack gave me a conducted tour, a demonstration, some samples, and snips from his extensive knowledge of a highly specialised trade. Established in 1911, the firm was a family business which applied engineering and blacksmithing techniques to clog iron making. Their finished products were bought by cloggers through grindery travellers.

Basically, irons were made from thin steel bars in which grooves were pressed. The grooves held the nails, which were countersunk through holes. Nail holes were punched rather than drilled. This and the shaping was done by improvised machines and caused some weakness in the iron, rendering it necessary for them to be annealed in a furnace before they were ready for use. Many of the machines were bought by Mr. Walkeley for his Huddersfield workshops, so they work on.

The history of Buck and Abbot's is interesting. Their manufacturing peak was between the two world wars, when they employed 40 people, though some trading was done in non-clog items. Latterly, the firm employed only three men. At the peak 16 tons of iron was used weekly but latterly only 35 tons a year. In the early days the owners would not agree to price fixing, so the clog trade tried to stop their production by getting iron manufacturers to stop supplying them. Buck and Abbot therefore went to Birmingham and set up a steel rolling mill — Dudley Port Rolling Mill, which is now part of the Ductile Group. There's ingenuity for you — a real case of Lancashire mettle! After the First World War, the French put a tariff on clog iron imports, so Mr Buck went to France and opened up a clog plant outside Tours. The family lived there for a couple of years before employing a manager. Lancashire's 'Captains of Industry' will not be beaten. The gavel in the Buck and Abbot boardroom was a clog iron.

Among the tricks employed by Buck and Abbot was that of making *fillers*, which were small irons to go in the centre of the outer irons so as to reduce sole wear. These were mostly used by quarry workers, and didn't wear out quickly, being of smaller gauge metal. An Accrington clogger, Jack Murray, told me of a similar trick of putting a clog iron, cut into two, between the outer irons. He further improvised by putting *side tins* or plates on the side of the sole to reduce wear caused by sliding.

Cloggers in North East Lancashire and the neighbouring West Riding would often order irons of a thicker gauge than usual, known as *Colne irons*. Silsden, near Keighley, was a village strong in clog iron and nail making tradition. Professor Moody visitied Silsden's clog iron smithies before they closed in 1950. He studied the speech and terms used there, recording the names of tools and processes. One unusual one was for the ends of the iron heel — *the nep*.

We know of course that pattens had an iron ring treader, but it appears that it wasn't until the 19th century that cloggers adapted the clog by providing it with an iron treader. Another word for treader is *caulker*, and what we call clog irons were originally known as caulkers (from the French *cauquer*: 'to tread') pronounced 'cokers'. I doubt if the clog would have survived as long as it did without the brilliance of invention that devised the caulker.

Basically, there have been only three designs of irons — commons, squares and duck toes. The last of these are extended toe-wards into a pointed shape. Squares fitted clogs of that shape, which were jokingly said to have been designed to enable the wearer to stand closer to the bar when drinking. Commons were just that — common-

place, ordinary. Little can be said about the differences in design of clog heel irons. Most of these have flattened ends, the purpose of this being that it would be bent over onto the heel edge or chamfer to give greater grip, though it was not always done. A clogger told me that the most common reason for irons coming off was the nail head wearing off.

Sizes in clogs are measured differently to shoes. A single size is larger than a shoe size. My size in shoes is 10, but in clogs it is 13. A clogger would have a size gauge, calibrated in both, and called his *size stick*. It is difficult to say just when clog soles were made into distinct left and right. The probability is that some sole cutters did make the difference obvious, whilst some cut exactly alike. Certainly, some cloggers even in the 1920s were cutting each one alike, just as had been done throughout history, but machines seem always to have cut lefts and rights. Previously, they were known as *straights*.

In 1941 the Government restricted supplies of upper leather to shoe manufacturers, and Clarks Shoe Makers began to experiment with wooden-soled shoes. Had clogs arrived back in fashionable circles? Clarks devised a flexible wooden sole, hinged at the tread to give pliability and comfort. Some 12% of their 1944 production of women's shoes were of this type, but it was discontinued as leather became more easily accessible after 1945. The cost of wooden soling was almost 25% greater than leather.

13.   Charity Begins at Home

THROUGHOUT the industrial north, clogs were for many years synonymous with poverty and hard work. Perhaps therein lies the reason for their rejection by the post-war public. In many towns there existed charitable funds administered by well-intentioned people anxious to provide poor folk, especially children, with clothing and footwear. I have come across memories of such bodies as the Chief Constable's Clothing Fund. Clogs issued by such bodies were often stamped 'Police' or 'Not to be Pawned' so that no pawnshop would accept them, on pain of criticism by the police inspecting the books and stock.

In Warton near Preston, under the will of Mary Southworth (1870), was set up the Southworth Trust for Poor Children. Invested money produced an income for the benefit of the local school and of deserving children. It is likely that, initially, all scholars would receive a pair of clogs each Christmas, but as the village grew they were limited to those having a full attendance. One lady told me, 'We were sent to school even if we were poorly to get the marks for clogs.' In 1885, the first distribution of 28 pairs, costing £3 11s 11d in total (2s 7d each), was made, rising by 1887 to 42, without increase. In 1903 a local clogger tendered prices for supplying the fund organiser:- A pair of size 6: 3s 2d; 5: 2s 11d;4: 2s 9d; 3: 2s 8d; 2: 2s 6d; 1: 2s 4d; 10: 2s.

The gift of clogs to all scholars finished about 1939, but in 1954 three deserving children received some supplied by Clegg's of Kirkham at a total cost of £2 15s 11d (two at 19s 6d; one at 16s 11d). Mrs Alice Simpson remembered 'Tom Clogger' making them in Freckleton, and that if boys wanted 'High up un's' they had to pay 6d or 9d extra themselves. In the 1880s the headmaster wrote in the fund notebook such comments as, 'Very deserving—father a labourer'; 'Five in school'; 'Half timer —works in mill'; 'Comes in all weathers'; and a note on the number of attendances. In 1973 the Charity Commissioners agreed to the Trustees of Warton School applying funds to the relieving of poor children of the parish in ways other than the provision of clogs.

In Burnley, a Clog Fund was run 'by the Town Hall'. Poor children were given a chit to hand to a clogger who then sent in a bill for clogs supplied. In Darwen at the time of the Cotton Famine a Relief Committee spent £30 5s 4d on clogs, this amount being shown separately in the accounts, thus indicating their importance. In Stockport at this time the Relief Fund distributed 19,000 pairs amongst some of the 30,500 living on charity. The town's population was only 55,000 then. As early as the end of the 17th century charity clogs were handed out at Worsley near Manchester.

So far as I am aware, there have been only two booklets previous to this one which have dealt solely with clogs. The first was a 34 page pamphlet, written and published about 1900 by Thomas Broughton, who was a wholesale clogger and block manufacturer.He ran his business in Warner Street, Accrington, and it exists today under the name of Thomas Yates, who bought it from Broughton. This business of 'wholesale leather and grindery merchants' is now run by two ladies. Broughton became Mayor of Accrington — I can imagine him wearing his clogs and ermine-trimmed robes. I wonder if he and Richard Turner of Clitheroe are the only cloggers to become mayors.

The other book is by Evelyn Vigeon, and is in fact an offprint of an essay she wrote for the Journal of the Costume Society 1977. She works for the Salford Museums Service, where the booklet is for sale, and has a long association with costume and clogs.

I close with a quote from Edwin Waugh, the finest of Lancashire dialect writers. In conversation, a 'sandknocker' (sand supplier) tells a customer, 'O ay, it'll be reet. Neaw tak care o' yorsel, an' keep your heart eawt o' yor clogs.' That goes for you too.

Bibliography

Amongst the books I have consulted have been the following, some of which I have referred to in the book by the author's name:

Vigeon, *Clogs or wooden soled shoes* (1977).

Broughton, *History of the Clog and Patten Trade* (n.d.).

Oakes & Hill, *Rural Costume: Its Origin and Development in Western Europe and the British Isles* (Batsford, 1970).

Edlin, *Woodland Crafts in Britain* (1949).

Jenkins, *Traditional country craftsmen.* (Routledge & Kegan Paul, 1965).

Wilson, *A history of shoe fashion* (Pitman, 1969).

Fitch, *The History of the Worshipful Company of Pattenmakers 1862/1926.*

Sulser, *A Brief History of the Shoe* (Bally Museum, 1958).

Ackworth, *Clog Shop Chronicles* (1896).

Clog Publicity Association, Clogs: *A valuable booklet for all who buy, wear and stock clogs.*

Mellor, *The Northern Music Hall.*

Fizrandolph & Hay, *The Timber and Woodland Industries and Some Village Workshops* (Oxford University Press, 1926).

Pilling, *The Lancashire Clog Dance* (E.F.D.S.S., 1967).

Bearman, *Poems in the Lancashire Dialect* (Dalesman, 1977).

Fairholt, *English Costume* (1846 and 1896).

Hartley, *Made in England* (1939).

Fletcher, *The Clatter of Clogs* (1972).

Wadsworth, *The Myth of the Flemish Weavers* (Rochdale Literary & Scientific Society, 1942).

Ormerod, *The Evolution of the English Clog* (The Footwear Organiser, 1921).

Sayce, *Pattens and Clogs* (Rochdale Literary & Scientific Society, 1943).

Woods, *The making of clogs, clog soles, clog blocks.* (Journal of Ministry of Agriculture, Nov. 1922).

Graham, *Lancashire and Cheshire Morris Dances* (1911).

Karpeles, *The Lancashire Morris* (E.F.D.S.S., 1930).

Wymer, *English Country Crafts* (Batsford).

Cunnington & Cunnington, *Handbook of English Costume in the 19th Century* (Faber, 1959).

Moody, *The nail and clog iron industries of Silsden in the West Riding* (Transactions of the Yorkshire Dialect Society, 1951).

*   *   *   *   *

See also:-

Atkinson, *Clogs & Clogmaking* (1984 Shire Publishing).

"Made to Last". Article on Jeremy Atkinson and clogmaking (Practical Woodworking, February 1993).

The Newcastle Series. 23 titles (to date) of clog-dancing interest published by INSTEP 15 Wolveleigh Terrace, Newcastle on Tyne. £2 each plus post.

Bibliography of clog & step dancing, compiled by Chris Metherell is soon to be published by E.F.D.S.S., Vaughan William Library, Cecil Sharp House, 2 Regents Park Road, London.

Clog Steps/Clog for Beginners/The Steps of Samuel Bell. 3 titles published 1981-4 by Mike Cherry £2 each. 3 Kibblewhite Crescent, Twyford, Berks. RG10 9AX.

Clog Dancing Made Easy. Henry Tucker (1874 USA). Reprinted 1989 by Chris Brady F31 Felbridge Court, 311 High Street, Harlington, Middx. UB3 5EP.

The Clog Maker; an account of clog making in Yorkshire & Lancashire around 1900. Leaflet published by Colne Valley Museum, Golcar, Huddersfield.

Barrand, *English Clog Dance Steps.* (1991 3rd Ed.) published by Morris Dance in America Press (Dr Anthony G. Barrand) University Professors Programme, The University, 745 Commonwealth Ave., Boston, Mass 02215. Dr. Barrand has also written and lectured extensively on clog and dance-related matters.

Hughes, *Clog Steps for Beginners* published by E.F.D.S.S.

Cloggers

No matter where your clogs were bought,
We can them repair.
And when you think they're fit for nought,
We'll make them fit to wear.

(An advertising jingle c. 1900)

Bill & Yvonne Turton, 129 High Street, Skelmersdale. (Shop also clog wholesalers). Tel: 0695 31678/23802.

Phillip Jones c/o Alston's, Unit 1, The Cattle Market, Brook Street, Preston (Shop. Clogs & Shoes). Tel: 0772 718309.

Rick Rybicki, Oxford House, Dale Street, Todmorden. (Shop. Clogs only.) Tel:

H. (Bert) Strain, 106 Pall Mall, Chorley. (Shop. Clogs & shoes). Tel: 0257 263010/278725.

Trefor Owen, Unit 28, Bolton Road Workshops, Wath on Dearne, Rotherham. (Workshop. Clogs only). Tel: 0709 877582

Jeremy Atkinson, Unit 1, Capuchin Yard, Church Street, Hereford. (Shop. Clogs & shoes). Tel: 0432 274269.

John Peters, 5/7 Walmesley Street, Rishton, Blackburn. (Shop. Clogs & shoes). Tel: 0254 887213.

Chris Cobbet t/a *"Cobbyclogs"*, 51 Elmwood, Astley Village, Chorley. (Workshop in his home. Part time on clogs only). Tel: 0257 267346.

Joe Horrocks, Manor Farm, Englesea Brook, Crewe, also The Workshop, White Lion Inn, Barthomley, near Crewe. (Part time on clogs only. Workshop). Tel: 0270 820332/882243.

Nelson's Footwear (Jim & Daniel), Duke Street, Settle. (Shop. Clogs, shoes & leather work). Tel: 072982 3523.

J. Strong & Son (Joe & Will), "Glen Cote", Upton, Caldbeck, Wigton. (Shop. Clogs & shoes). Tel: 06998 424.

Galloway Footwear (Godfrey Smith & Nikki Finch), The Clog & Shoe Workshop, Balmaclellan, Galloway (Shop. Clogs & shoes). Tel: 06442 465.

Nelson Bailey, 67 Main Street, Galgate, Lancaster. (Shop. Clogs & Shoes). Tel: 0524 752600/752277.

Colne Valley Museum Cloggers, Cliffe Ash, Golcar, Huddersfield HD7 4PY. (6 volunteer cloggers in museum workshop, demonstrating & teaching Have produced *"The Clogmaker"* leaflet. Open Saturday and Sunday 2 p.m. - 5 p.m. & midweek groups). Tel: 0484 659762.

Malcolm Huggett, 28 Mayflower Drive, Yateley, Camberley, Surrey. (Part-time from home workshop. Clogs only). Tel: 0252 879788.

Allan Roberts, Chapel Gate Farm, Winewall, Trawden, Colne BB8 8BS. (Part-time, clogs only, Home workshop). Tel: 0282 871991.

Scarab Clogs (Mik Howard), c/o "Oblivion", 14 South Gallery, Exchange St., Sheffield S2 5TR. (Workshop within a shop). Tel: 0742 766234.

Jacal Clogs (John Loughlin), 21 London St., Newport, Gwent NP9 8DW. (Part-time from home workshop. Clogs only). Tel: 0633 246857.

Phil Howard, 16 Lowside Ave., Woodley, Stockport SK6 1JU. (Part-time from home. Clogs & other leather Morris items). Tel: 061 494 0224.

Bryan Speak, 22 Woone Lane, Clitheroe, Lancs. (Shop. Full-time Clogs & shoes). Tel: 0200 28530.

Ellis Greenwood, 80 Haworth Road, Cross Roads, Keighley BD22 9DL. (Shop. Clogs & shoes). Tel: 0535 644537 (Evenings)

Walkley's, Canal Wharf Sawmills, Burnley Road, Hebden Bridge, HX7 8NH. (Large premises manufacturing, retailing and wholesaling clogs as well as being a tourist attraction, open every day of the year). Tel: 0422 842061.

Dandy Clogs (John the Fish), 2 Tarrandean Bungalows, Perranwell Station, Truro. TR3 7NP. (Home Workshop. Part-time on clogs & leather goods). Tel: 0872 863825.

Walter Hurst, 4 Wigan Road, Hindley, Wigan. (Shop. Full-time. Clogs & shoes). Tel: 0942 55531.

Bruce Haw, Northampton House, Aysgarth, Leyburn, North Yorkshire DL28 3AH. (Part-time from home workshop. Clogs only). Tel: 0969 663250.

Hywel Davies, 60 Ninian Road, Roath, Cardiff. (Part-time workshop in Welsh Folk Museum, Cardiff. Clogs only). Tel: 0222 569441/4733244.

Winfield Shoe Company, Hazel Mill, Blackburn Road, Haslingden, Rossendale. (Shoe retailers with full-time clogger). Tel: 0706 227916.

*   *   *   *   *

Most of the cloggers listed are members of The Guild of Traditional Clog Makers. The Secretaries are Bill & Yvonne Turton, 129 High Street, Skelmersdale. Tel: 0695 31678/23802.

Teachers of Clog Dancing

Here is a list of clog dancers who also teach step-clog. It is as accurate as I have found it possible to be, though I realise it is by no means complete. Good advice for anyone wishing to learn to clog dance would be to contact one of the groups (see the separate list) involved in it, as a great deal of teaching is done within groups. Those names marked with a * have been recently confirmed as active teachers, those marked with a + have not.

* Chris Metherell, 15 Wolveleigh Terrace, Newcastle on Tyne NE3 1UP. Tel: 091 284 1259. Teacher and heads a team of dance researchers who publish clogs-related books known collectively as The Newcastle Series. 23 in series so far. The team is called The Instep Research Team.

* Penny Smith, 48 Lime Tree Ave., Retford, Notts. DN22 7BA. Tel: 0777 703837.

* Kirsty Higgs, 63 Doxey Fields, Doxey, Stafford ST16 1HJ. Tel. 0785 45522. Pro for West Midland Folk Federation.

* Christine Fitt, Glendevon, Shepherd Lane, Thurnscoe, Rotherham S63 0JS. Tel: 0709 894347.

* David Smith, 37 School Street, Farington, Leyland, PR5 2QB. Tel: 0772 457642.

* Ann Smith, The Old Bakery, Coleford, Bath BA3 5PB. Tel: 0373 812227.

* Alex Woodcock, 290b Flathurst Cottages, Horsham Road, Petworth, GU28 OHB. Tel: 0798 43879.

* May and Harold Ross, 36 Church Street, Langford, Biggleswade SG18 9QT. Tel: 0462 700164.

* Alex Boydell, Hillview, Salwayash, Bridport, Dorset DT6 5HU. Tel: 0308 88456.

* Liza Austin, Fosbrook Cottage, 2 Hightate Road, Hayfield, Derbs. SK12 5JL. Tel: 0663 746089.

* Jane Pollitt, 1 Moreton Lane, Offerton, Stockport. Tel: 061 456 8645.

* Carys Reckless, 13 Coppice Lane, Poynton, Cheshire. Tel: 0625 871332.

* Rachel Calderbank, 154 Wigan Road, Euxton, Chorley PR7 6JW. Tel: 0257 269397.

* Jacqui & Cath Bayliss, 428 Croston Road, Leyland PR5 3PJ. Tel: 0772 455877.

* Gwen Naylor, 20 Lords Lane, Huddersfield Road, Brighouse HD6 3RF.

* Brenda Walker, Court Inn, Court Lane, Durham City DH1 3AW. Tel: 091 3860714.
* Alan Whittaker, 81 St. Anne's Road, Leyland, Preston PR5 2XR. Tel: 0772 431640.
* Mike Cherry, 3 Kibblewhite Crescent, Twyford, Berks. RG10 9AX. Tel. 0734 321326. Teaches & publishes clog dancing books.
* Ian Dunmur, Croft House Farm, Mosedale, Mungrisdale, Penrith, CA11 0XQ.
* John Walford, 53 Cressingham Road, Reading, RG2 7RX. Tel: 0734 874767.
* Laurie Mulliner, 14 Wentworth Crescent, Hayes, Middx. UB3 1NL. Tel: 081 573 4327.
* Melanie Barber, 6 Youngs Road, Barkingside, Essex. 1G2 7LF. Tel: 081 518 5787.
* Chas Fraser, 42 Douglas Road, Worsley, Manchester M28 4SG. Tel: 061 794 7594.
* Harry Cowgill, Eagle's Nest, Brindle, Chorley PR6 8NS. Tel: 0254 852907.
* Virginia Crewe, 38 Chatburn Park Drive, Brierfield, Nelson BB9 5QA. Tel: 0282 698455.
* Doreen & Charles Sparey, 'Waterside', Lower Anderton Road, Millbrook, Cornwall PL10 1DN. Tel: 0752 822375.
* Tony, Marguerite & Jennifer Hill, 2 Birch Cottage, Werneth Low, Hyde, Cheshire SK14 3AD. Tel: 061 368 2742.
* Pat Tracey, Langlands, Lt. Braxted, Witham, Essex CM8 3LD. Tel: 0621 891535.
* Wendy Crouch, 10 Butchers Close, Bishops Itchington, Warwicks CV33 0PX. Tel: 0926 613648.
* Madeleine Smith, 51 Elderdene, Chinnor 0X9 4EJ. Tel: 0844 352468.
* Catherine Goss, 24 Nun Street, Lancaster LA1 3PJ. Tel: 0524 36671.
* Juliet Abson & Ed Daw, 38 Derwent Road, Lancaster. Tel: 0524 60877.
* Jane & Anthony Lepp, 17 Woodsmoor Lane, Stockport SK2 7AS.
+ Doug & Fiona Smith, 32 The Cheethams, Blackrod, Bolton BL6 5RR. Tel: 0942 832911.
* Sam Sherry, 53 Meadow Park, Galgate, Lancaster LA2 0NH. Tel: 0524 751785.
* Deborah Kermode, 60 Soutergate, Ulverston, LA12 7ES. Tel: 0229 52704.
* Tessa De Ville, 4 Sycamore Road, East Leake, Loughborough, LE12 6PS. Tel: 0509 852189.

* Glynis Cheers, The Street, Manuden, Bishops Stortford, Herts. Tel: 0279 812165.

+ Doris Hawkes, 9 Welbank Road, Usworth, Washington NE37 2TP.

* Gay Bettinson, 22 Main Street, St. Bees, Cumbria. Tel: 0946 823997

* Theresa Hindle, 38 Laburnum Drive, Oswaldtwistle, Accrington BB5 3AW. Tel: 0254 383602.

* Deborah Riley, 15 Reith Way, Accrington. Tel: 0254 383602.

* Tiffany Searle, 14 Thame Road, Haddenham, Aylesbury HP17 8EW. Tel: 0844 291015. Teaches & dances with a partner as *"The Itinerant Cloggies"*.

* Sue Jenkinson, 17 St. James Close, Sutton on Hull, N. Humberside. Tel: 0482 878658.

* Lynette Eldon, 129 Westcott Street, Holderness Road, Hull HU8 8NB. Tel: 0482 703261.

* Joan Holloway, 102 London Road, Whitchurch, Hants RG28 7LT. Tel: 0256 896987.

* Faye Dillon, Nirth End Cottage, Kingston Winslow, Ashby, Wilts. Tel: 0793 710252.

* Jacqueline Wright, 15 Blenheim Way, Horspath, Oxford. Tel: 0865 774423.

+ Angela Lee, Lea Field, Craw Hall, Brampton, Cumbria CA8 1TL.

* Chris Brady, F31 Felbridge Court, 311 High Street, Harlington, Middx UB3 5EP. Tel: 081 897 1700.

* Lynn Colbeck, 64 Greenfield Crescent, Cowplain, Waterlooville, Hants PO8 9EJ. Tel: 0705 599065. Organises *"Mayfly"* dance workshops.

* Irene Thompson, 24 Langdon Street, Sheffield S11 8BJ. Tel: 0742 580535.

* Linda Burton, 56 Bellingham Road, Kendal LA9 5JP. Tel: 0539 733086.

* Ian Craigs, 8 Tempest Street, Stella, Blaydon-on-Tyne NE21 4ND. Tel: 091 414 1863.

* Alex Fisher, 84 Featherstone Road, Newton Hall, Durham City DH1 5YP. Tel: 091 386 2554.

+ Jane Lloyd, 15 The Northern Road, Crosby, Liverpool.

* Gill Barraclough, 21 Southern Road, Sale, Cheshire. Tel: 061 969 0288.

* Karen Gilsenan, 10 Richmond Avenue, Handford, Wilmslow SK9 3JB. Tel: 0625 536089.

* Huw Williams, 1 Tudor Crescent, Brynmawr, Gwent. Tel: 0495 311239.

* Heather Bexton, 19 St. Peter's Close, Stowmarket IP14 1LF. Tel: 0449 615816.

* Pam Ross, Southview, Common Road, Shelfanger, Diss IP22 2DP. Tel: 0379 643563.

* Jane Vipond, Prospect Cottage, Aislaby Road, Eaglescliffe, Cleveland TS16 0JJ. Tel: 0642 787280.

* Ed Wilson, 1 Greenfield Place, Ryton, Tyne & Wear. Tel: 091 413 4633.

* Foss, The Coach House, Eden, Banff AB45 3NT. Tel: 02616 220.

* Lis Price, 49 Sanderling Road, Offerton, Stockport SK2 5UL. Tel: 061 427 6651.

+ Ronnie Collis, 40 Lumbertub Lane, Boothville, Northampton NN3 1AH. Tel: 0604 643408.

* John Walford, 53 Cressingham Road, Reading RG2 7RX. Tel: 0734 874767.

* Laurie Mulliner, 14 Wentworth Crescent, Hayes, Middx UB3 1NL. Tel: 081 573 4327.

+ Sue Mycock, Green Garth, Old Brackenland, Wigton, Cumbria. Tel: 06973 44363.

+ David & Audrey Anderton, 16 Croxteth Drive, Rainford, St. Helens WA11 8JZ.

* Sue Bousfield, 7 The Hermitage, Thorton-Cleveleys FY5 2TH. Tel: 0253 822089.

* Geoff Hughes, 87 Stratton Drive, Platt Bridge, Wigan. Tel: 0942 861084.

* Terry Kelly, 120 Walmer Road, Pakefield, Lowestoft NR33 7LD. Tel: 0502 566434.

Groups who dance in clogs

Here is a list, in rough alphabetical order, of groups of people who wear clogs when dancing. In the main, these fall into two sorts - those who step-dance together, and those who do Morris-type dancing. I have tried to show a group's name, it's contact person, and which sort of dancing they (either males, females or mixed sexes) perform. Most of the Morris dancing is of the North West style. Those marked * have recently confirmed as *"information corrrect"*, but those marked + have not been so confirmed. Whilst there are lists of dance sides/groups/teams (various names are applied) so far as I can ascertain none of the published lists detail whether the participants dance in clogs or shoes. I hope that one of the listing agencies will taken this as a suggestion.

Anyone wishing to make contact with those bodies to which groups belong should consider contacting the main ones:-

English Folk Dance & Song Society (E.F.D.S.S.), Cecil Sharp House, 2 Regents Park Road, London NW1 7AY. Tel: 071 485 2206.

Open Morris, Mike Salter, Folly Cottage, 151 West Malvern Road, Malvern WR14 4AY. Tel: 0684 565211.

The Morris Ring, Chas Arnold, 13 Belper Road, Kilburn, Derby. Tel: 0332 881404.

The Morris Federation, Beth Neill, 36 Foxbury Road, Bromley, Kent BR1 4DQ. Tel: 081 460 0623.

+ Argarmales Morris, Linda Corcoran, 16 Croxteth Drive, Rainford, St. Helens WA11 8JZ.

* Addison Rapper & Clog Dance Team, Ian Wilson, 27 Wallace Street, Spital Tongues, Newcastle on Tyne NE2 4AU. Tel: 091 232 4329.

+ Annie's Fantasies, Martin Lawson, 4 Leicester Close, Colchester, Essex.

+ Anstey Royale Chalfont, Christine Burnett, 33 Waterfield Road, Cropston, Leics. LE7 7HL.

+ All Fools Morris & Clog, Brian Connors, 4 Bryn Llys, Capel Curig, Gwynedd LL24 0EF. Tel: 06904 245.

* Basingclog Morris, Roger & Jill Wheble, 6 Brambling Close, Kempshott, Basingstoke RG22 5JX. Tel: 0256 25207. Mixed.

* Bangles, Beads & Bloomers, Virginia Crewe, Park High School, Colne, Lancs. BB8 7DP. Tel: 0282 865200/698455. Junior Girls Morris.

* Bollin Morris, Trevor Johnson, 22 Lorraine Road, Timperley, Altrincham, Cheshire. Tel: 061 980 6731. Mixed.

* Britannia Coco-nut Dancers, Derek Pilling, 31 Booth Road, Waterfoot, Rossendale, Lancs. BB4 9BQ. Tel: 0707 218003. Men's Morris. Their year's highspot is on Easter Saturday in Bacup's streets.

* Beetlecrushers, Ann Smith, The Old Bakery, Coleford, Bath BA3 5PB. Tel: 0373 812227. Women Step-dancers.

* Benskins Morris, Peter Cotton, 25 The Meadow Way, Harrow Weald, Harrow HA3 7BP. Tel: 081 863 7898. Mixed. Morris.

* Black Adder Rapper & Step, Sally Atkinson, 70 Station Road, Shepley, Huddersfield HD8 8DU. Tel: 0484 605059. Ladies.

* Bobbins & Reelers, Margaret Cannon, Cragg Nook, Cocker Hill, Foulridge, Colne BB8 7LW. Tel: 0282 867856. Ladies Morris.

* Bon Accord Cloggies, Jane Ferguson, 90 Clifton Road, Aberdeen AB2 3RJ. Tel: 0224 491696. Ladies Step-dancers.

* Bows 'n' Belles, Sheila Boxshall, 73 Keable Road, Marks Tey, Colchester CO6 1XR. Tel: 0206 211498. Ladies Morris.

* Bury Pace-eggers, Alan Seymour, 166 Tottington Road, Tottington, Bury BL8 1RU. Tel: 061 761 1544.

+ Briggate Morris, Mary Burgess, 7 Kirk Drive, Baildon, BD17 6SA. Women.

* Barley Break Ladies Folk Dancers, Hilary de Wit, Carrier's Cottage, 18 North Kelsey Road, Casitor, Lincs. LN7 6QN. Tel: 0472 851159. Ladies Morris.

* Barley Brigg Morris, Jill Parson, Bell Corner, Owl's Green, Laxfield, Road, Dennington, Woodbridge IP13 8BX. Tel: 0728 75293. Mixed.

+ Broomfield Clog, Brenda Gurnham, 22 Juliet Close, Nuneaton, CV4 9DG.

* Colne Royal Morris Men, Julian Pilling, 126 Railway Street, Nelson BB9 9AL. Tel: 0282 698366.

* Charnwood Clog, Joan Harris, 17 Pope Street, Leicester LE2 6DX. Tel: 0533 703492. Step dance side.

* Clever Clogs, Gwen Jones, 161 Stockport Road, Marple, SK6 6DN. Tel: 0663 743238. Ladies step dancers.

* Carnkie Cloggers, Helen Gambier, 1 Crowan Cottage, Crowan, Helston, Cornwall. Tel: 0209 831899. Morris.

* Young Colne Lads, Frank Warrington, Park High School, Venables Avenue, Colne BB8 7DP. Tel: 0282 865200. Junior Morris.

* Craven Flagcrackers, Sandra Roberts, Chapel Gate Farm, Winewall, Trawden, Colne BB8 8BS. Tel: 0282 871991. Mixed Morris.

* Chesterfield Garland Dancers, Lyn Pardo, 22 Stanley Street, Spital, Chesterfield S41 0EZ. Tel: 0246 220741. Ladies.

* Cat Nab Clog Dancers, Jane Brown, 4 Windy Hill Lane, Marske By The Sea, Redcar, Cleveland TS11 7BN. Tel: 0642 476802. Ladies Step dancers.

* Cobbler's Awl, Carol Loughlin, 21 London Street, Newport, Gwent NP7 8DW. Tel: 0633 246857. Mixed. Step-dancers.

* Carlisle Sword Morris & Clog, Jeff Lawson, Cairnbridge Barn, Heads Nook, Carlisle, Cumbria CA3 9EH. Tel: 0228 561457/0434 381226. Mixed.

* Camden Clog, Pat Tracey, Langlands, Lt. Braxted, Witham, Essex. CM8 3LD. Tel: 0621 891535. Mixed Step-dancers.

* Cantwara, Phil Edmunds, 44 Wincheap, Canterbury CT1 3RS. Tel: 0227 766073. Mixed Step-dancers.

+ Clitheroe Country Fayre Morris, Julie Johnson, 66 Palmer Road, Blackburn BB1 8BS.

+ Clitheroe Morris Men, Hans Van Dyke, 52 Moorland Crescent, Clitheroe.

+ Cheshire Cloghoppers, Jennie Shaw, 6 Brisbane Close, Bramhall, Stockport.

+ Cheshire Royal Morris, Eileen Shepherd, 3 Swanwick Close, Goosetree, Crewe.

+ Chester City Men, Allan Jones, 19 Boughton Hall Drive, Gt. Boughton, Chester CH3 5QG.

+ Chorlton Green Morris, 16 Brixton Avenue, Withington, Manchester M20 8JF.

+ Crosskey Clog, Christine Stevenson, 195 Mayor's Walk, Peterborough, PE3 7HG. Tel: 0733 61518.

* Cockleshell Clog, Derek Oliver, 148 Essex Way, South Benfleet, Essex SS7 1LN. Tel: 0268 794556/296423. Mixed Morris.

+ Codlins & Cream, Mrs Starkey, 49 Tennyson Road, Maldon, Essex.

+ Cotton Mill Clog Morris, Bob Coombes, 38 Castle Road, St. Albans, Herts.

+ Chelmsford Ladies Morris, Liz Day, 124 Lymington Avenue, Leigh on Sea SS9 2AN. Tel: 0702 710053.

+ Clydeside Clog, G. Kirk, 108 McGregor Road, Cumbernauld, G67 1JM.

* Claygate Cloggies, Fay Jenkins, 387 Kingston Road, Ewell KT19 0BS. Tel: 081 394 1361. Mixed Step-dancers.

+ Cleveland Clog, C. Burnett, 14 Spennithorne Road, Stockton, Cleveland. Tel: 0642 607860.

* Cloggers Row, Jean Tomlinson, 8 Hill End Grove, Bradford BD7 4RP. Tel: 0274 571074. Mixed Step-dancers.

+ Chestnut Cloggies, Deborah Melmoth, 24 Windsor Close, Cleveden, Avon. BS21 5EW. Tel: 0272 874393.

+ Cloghoppers, Shirley Taylor, 23 Avondale Road, Fleet, Hants. GU13 9BH. Tel: 0252 628190.

* The Double-Legged Roundhouse Backsliders, (The Backsliders), Cathy Goss, 24 Nun Street, Lancaster LA1 3PJ. Tel: 0524 36671. Mixed Step dancers.

* Dorset Buttons Morris Side, Lillian Connor, 25 Rushcombe Way, Wimborne, BH21 3QR. Tel: 0202 693863. Female Morris and Male Rapper.

* Duke's Dandy Clog, Penny Smith, 48 Lime Tree Avenue, Retford, Notts. DN22 7BA. Tel: 0777 703837. Ladies Step-dance team.

* Devils Jumps, Ann Moore, 7 Summerhill Road, Cowplain, Hants. PO8 8XD. Tel: 0705 251225. Mixed Step-dancers.

+ Dandy Clog, Heather Newton, Touchwood, 9 Wood View, Penrhyn, TR10 8QA.

+ Devon Oak Clog Dancers, Barbara Chambers, Meadow View, Clyst Hydon, Cullompton, EX15 2ND.

+ Danegeld, B. Prettyman, 37 Ruskin Road, Ipswich, IP4 1PT.

* Dublin City Morris Dancers, Frances Tuffery, 9 Grange Park Avenue, Dublin 5, Ireland. Tel: 010 353 1 8480941. Mixed.

+ Eaglesfield Paddlers, Mike Breese, Highfield House, Deanscales, Cockermouth CA13 0SN.

* Fosbrook's Stockport Premier Morris Dancers, Liza Austin, Fosbrook Cottage, 2 Highgate Road, Hayfield SK12 5JL. Tel: 0663 746089.

* Fylde Coast Cloggers, Doris Evans, 50 Westby Street, Lytham St. Annes FY8 5JG. Tel: 0253 730991. Ladies Morris.

* Fiddlesticks, Jill Bazire, The Homestead, Three Hammer Common, Neatishead, Norfolk NR12 8BP. Tel: 0692 630755. Ladies Morris.

* Fen Nightingales, Margaret Lambert, 14 Ivatt Street, Cottenham, Cambs. CB3 4SJ. Tel: 0954 50609. Ladies Step-dancers.

+ Fidlers Fancy Women's Morris, Barbara Knight, 68 Ogden Road, Bramhall, Stockport. SK7 1NH.

* Furness Clog Dancers, Deborah Kermode, 60 Soutergate, Ulverston LA12 7ES. Tel: 0229 52704. Ladies Step-dancers.

+ Fidlers Brook, Sally Ovenden, 13 Delfield, Anchor Lane, Wadesmill, New Ware, Herts.

+ Frithwoods Clog, L. Woollacott, Tricket Gate House, Tricket Bridge, Catsleton, Sheffield. Tel: 0298 71696.

+ First Light Ladies Morris, Beth Kelly, 120 Walmer Road, Lowestoft NR33 7LD. Tel. 0502 566434.

* Grenoside Sword Dancers, Ray Ellison, 3 Grenogate, Grenoside, Sheffield S30 3NY. Tel: 0742 453361. Men.

* Garstang Morris Dancers, David Nussey, 11 The Boulevard, Lytham St. Annes, FY8 1EH. Tel: 0253 723159. Men.

* Green Ginger Clog Dancers, Sue Jenkinson, 17 St. James Close, Sutton on Hull, N. Humberside. Tel: 0482 878658. Ladies Step-dance side.

* Great Central Clog, Lesley Robson, 40 Grasmere Close, Rugby CV21 1LS. Tel: 0788 562418. Ladies Step-dancers.

* Gyppeswyck Garland, Lorraine Jarman, Lothlorien, Stone Street, Crowfield, Ipswich IP6 9SY. Tel: 0449 79241. Female Morris & Step-dancers.

* Greenwood Step Clog Dancers, Dorothy Martin, 120 Long Lane, Attenborough, Nottingham NG9 6BW. Tel: 0602 221244. Ladies.

+ Gorton Morrismen, John Kirk, 8 Church Street, Bollington, Cheshire.

* Original Garstang Morris Men, Roger Westbrook, Kerry Cottage, 1 Lane Ends, Sabden, Blackburn BB6 9EZ. Tel: 0282 779335.

+ Green Willow Clog, Jane Taylor, Cheney Cottage, Broadhempston, Totnes. TQ9 6BD.

* Hertfordshire Holly, Barbara Jeffery, 21 Greenstead, Sawbridgenorth, CM21 9NY. Tel: 0279 723090. Ladies Morris.

* Horberie Shroggies - see Wakefield Morris

* Haughley Hoffers, Sally Taylor, 1 Danes Close, Stowmarket, Suffolk IP14 1QJ. Tel: 0449 677342. Ladies Morris.

* Hoxon Hundred, Ron & Pam Ross, Southview, Common Road, Shelfanger, Diss IP22 2DP. Tel: 0379 643563. Mixed, Men's & Ladies' Morris.

* Harrow Cloggies, John Lawes, 29 Tenby Avenue, Harrow HA3 8RU. Tel: 081 907 4700. Organisers of an annual (3rd Saturday in May) Clog & Step Dance Festival. Mixed group of individual step dancers.

* Horwich Prize Medal Morris, Bob Bradley, 15 Shrewsbury Road, Bolton BL1 4NW. Tel: 02024 840949. Men's N.W.

* Handforth Morris, Keith Boulton, 51 Drummond Way, Macclesfield, SK10 4XJ. Tel: 0625 829280. Mixed.

* Hellath Wen, Jane Bevan, 3 Bray Close, Crewe CW1 1LJ. Tel: 0270 589286. Ladies Morris.

+ Hoddesdon Crownsmen, S. Heath, 56 West Road, Stanstead Mount, Fitchet, Essex CM24 8NQ.

* Hartshead Morris, Dave Ellam, 14 Ferncroft, High Town, Liversedge, WF15 8DT. Tel: 0274 873980. Mixed.

+ Hungerford Clog Side, Joanna Debono, 37 Priory Avenue, Hungerford RG17 0BE.

+ Heather & Gorse, Jackie Lake, 6 Avenue Road, Kings Kerswell, Devon.

+ Hampshire Garland, Mrs Miller, 44 Stoneham Lane, Swaythling, Southampton.

* Hart & Sole Clog Morris, Adrian Groves, 31 Corrine Close, Whitley Wood, Reading RG2 8AA. Tel: 0734 872073. Mixed.

+ Hedge Betty, Ruth Taylor, 1 Falcon Close, Kidderminster, DY10 1NN.

* Hips & Haws, Lyn Stevenson, 17 Tugela Road, Chippenham, Wilts SN15 1JF. Tel. 0249 659237. Ladies Morris & Step.

+ Island Cloggies, D. Goodenough, Hazelmere, Shide Path, Newport, Isle of Wight PO30 1HJ. Tel: 0983 528910.

+ John O'Gaunt Morrismen, 10 Gloucester Aven, Lancaster LA1 4ES.

+ Jenny Geddes Clog, C. Shearing, 17 Royal Park Terrace, Edinburgh.

* Kern Morris, Jim McCaffery, 7 Hillcrest, Gilesgate, Durham City DH1 1RB. Tel: 091 386 8149. Mixed.

* Kebles Queen Clog Team, Maura Booth, 65 Chapel Street, Wath on Dearne, Rotherham S63 7RL. Tel: 0709 875910. Ladies Step dancers.

+ Knaresborough Mummers, Doug Child, 6 Carr Manor Gardens, Leeds. Tel: 0532 686910.

+ Kettle Bridge Clogs, Sandra Sharp, 93 Glebe Lane, Barming, Maidstone ME16 9BA.

* Knockhundred Shuttles Clog Morris, Marian Hakeman, Well Cottage, Steep Marsh, Petersfield GU32 2BS. Tel: 0730 892777. Mixed.

+ Kendal Brewery Hops, Nicola Hunter, 81 Greengate, Levens LA8 8NF.

+ Knightwood Oak Clog, Phil Rothwell, 19 Pemberton Road, Lyndhurst, Hants.

* Kirkburton Rapier Dancers, Gary Stringfellow, 86 Wharf Street, Sowerby Bridge, HX6 2AF. Tel: 0422 833862. Men.

* Lancashire Rose Morris, Rachel Calderbank, 154 Wigan Road, Euxton, Chorley PR7 6JW. Tel: 0257 269397. Ladies.

* Lancashire Wallopers, Alan Whittaker, 81 St. Anne's Road, Leyland PR5 2XR. Tel: 0772 431640. Mixed step-dancers. Organise an annual clog festival.

* Leyland Morris Men, Geoff Carson, 13 Yewlands Avenue, Fulwood, Preston PR2 4QR. Tel: 0772 712199.

* Leopard Spot, Sue Shore, 29 Hope Street, Bignall End, Stoke on Trent ST7 8PX. Tel: 0782 7217660. Ladies step-dancers.

* Liberty Bell Clog Dancers, Christine Fitt, Glendevon, Sherherd Lane, Thurnscoe, Rotherham S63 0JS. Tel: 0709 894347 or 0302 707762. Mixed Step dancers.

* Little Piecers, Margaret Cannon, Cragg Nook, Cocker Hill, Foulridge. Colne. BB8 7LW. Tel: 0282 867856. Junior Mixed Morris.

+ Lancashire Folly, Wendy Binns, 31 Augusta Close, Rochdale OL12 6HT.

+ Langford Clog, Harold & May Ross, 36 Church Street, Langford, Biggleswade SG18 9QT. Tel: 0462 700164.

* Longshaw Morris, Beth Kelly, 120 Walmer Road, Pakefield, Lowestoft NR33 7LD. Tel: 0502 566434. Mixed.

* Minster Clog, Maureen Goring, 38 Sambourne Road, Warminster, Wilts. BA12 8LG. Tel: 0985 218217. Ladies. Step-dancers, esp. North East.

* Mayflower Morris, Myrtle Cooper, 3 Churt Wynde, Hindhead, Surrey. Tel: 0428 606495. Ladies. Morris.

* Manley Morris Dancers, Steve Ikin, 1 The Drive, Holmes Chapel CW4 7BJ. Tel: 0477 534785. Men's Morris.

* Mr Wilkins' Shilling, Kate Rawlings, 6 Stonehouse Close, Combe Down, Bath BA2 5DP. Tel: 0225 834716. Ladies Morris.

+ Manchester Morrismen, John Edge, 2 Buckland, Salford M6 8GP.

* Milltown Cloggies, Brenda Bonner, 85 Bradley Green Road, Hyde SK14 4LY. Tel: 061 366 5664. Female Morris.

+ Mossley Morris Men, John Squirrel, 46 Tib Street, Denton M34 1EN.

+ Minden Rose, Mrs Long, 40 Wootey's Way, Alton, Hants. GU34 2LD.

+ Manor Mill Morris, Julia Searby, 28 Park Road, Sawston, Cambs CB2 4TA.

+ Mill On The Brook Morris, Lesley Weeks, 11 Molesworth Terrace, Mill Brook, Torpoint, Cornwall.

+ Mandrake Morris, Liz Bruce, 55 Station Street, Walton on Naze CO14 8DW.

+ Magog Morris, M. Lyttleton, 13 Coney Close, Langley Green, Crawley, RH11 7QA.

* Mossley Rose & Clog Mixed Morris, Alison Dean, 18 Queensway, Greenfield, Oldham OL3 7AH. Tel: 0457 870391.

* Nook Morris, Crompton, Phelyp Bennett, 128 Beal Lane, Crompton OL2 8PH. Tel: 0706 847630. Mixed.

* Nottingham Pride, Marion Smalley, 10 Whitby Crescent, Woodthorpe, Nottingham NG5 4LY. Tel: 0602 263562/782707. Mixed Morris.

* Norwich Clog, Sylvia Hughes 7 Parmenter Close, Aylsham, Norfolk NR11 6AX. Tel: 0263 733448. Ladies step-dancers.

* Newcastle Cloggies, Alice Metherell, 15 Wolveleigh Terrace, Newcastle On Tyne NE3 1UP. Tel: 091 284 1259. Mixed step-dancers.

+ Naked Man Morris, Mrs Sutherland, 70 Queen Katherine Road, Lymington SO41 9RZ.

+ Nancy Butterfly, Linda Boswell, 14 Welcombe Drive, Warmley, Sutton Coldfield B76 8ND.

+ Old Meg Ladies Morris, Ann Lewis, Meadowbank, Picken End, Hanley Swan WR8 0DQ.

* Ossy Cloggers, Pat Boyle, 2 Hartley Street, Oswaldtwistle, Accrington BB5 3NQ. Tel: 0254 397799. Junior Mixed. Morris & Step.

* Offcumduns, Heather Inkpen, 20 Hargate, Littleborne, Canterbury. Tel: 0227 720529. Mixed Morris.

+ Old Palace Clog, D. Symes, Flat B, 9 Whitehorse Lane, S. Norwood, London SE25 6RD.

* Old Tanglefoot Clog, Joan Holloway, 102 London Road, Whitchurch Hants. RG28 7LT. Tel: 0256 896987. Step-dancers.

+ Pump House Clog Morris, Lesley Bradshaw, 25 Judge Street, Watford WD2 5AN. Tel: 0923 243061.

* Peg Leg Unicorn, Hilary McNamara, 17 Nursery Road, Bishops Stortford, Herts. CM23 3HJ. Tel: 0279 656664. Ladies Step-dancers.

* Preston Royal Morris Dancers, John McAlister, 339 Chapel Lane, New Longton, Preston PR4 4AA. Tel: 0772 612531. Men.

* Persephone, Ruth Wynne, 16 Farnley Lane, Otley LS21 2AB. Tel: 0943 462420. Ladies Morris.

* Pennyroyal, Kay Mills, 28 Marchmont Road, Wallington, Surrey SM6 9NU. Tel: 081 395 5945. Women Step-dancers.

+ Poynton Jemmers, Lizzie Jackson, 39 Broomfield Road, Heaton Mersey, Stockport.

+ Pendragon Morris, 9 Kenmore Way, Cleckheaton BD19 3EL.

+ Plymouth Maids, Rosamund Twinn, Landsdowne, Walkhampton, Yelverton, Devon.

+ Palatine Clog Morris, Mrs Ryder, 6 Marshall Terrace, Gilesgate Moor, Durham.

+ Panhaggerty Ladies Morris, Mrs Coates, 71 Woodlands Terrace, Darlington.

+ Quayside Cloggies, Chris Sparkes, 2 Courthill Road, Parkstone, Poole.

* Ripon City Morris Dancers, Ted Dodsworth, Neresforde, Skelding, Grantley, Ripon. Tel: 0765 620374. Men's Morris.

* Ring O' Belles - see Wakefield Morris Dancers.

* Rainbow Morris, Mrs Jo Buck, 7 Hilton Drive, Shipley BD18 2AL. Tel: 0274 593030/568596. Ladies.

* Ragged Staff, Wendy Crouch, 10 Butchers Close, Bishops Itchington, Warwicks CV33 0PX. Tel: 0926 613648. Mixed Clog Stepping.

* Ringheye Morris of Mobberley, Julie Solomons, 17 Randle Bennett Close, Elworth, Sandbach CW11 9GA. Tel: 0270 760603 or 0625 515053. Mixed Morris.

* Rochdale Morris, Kate Dixon, 24D Albert Avenue, Prestwich, Manchester M25 8LX. Tel: 061 773 0078. Mixed.

* Reading Cloggies, Marian Targett, 35 Somerton Gardens, Earley, Reading. Tel: 0734 862393. Mixed Step-dancers. Organise an annual clog festival. A very active group.

* Ripley Green Garters, Ronda Sims, 5 Hawkins Drive, Ridgeway, Ambergate, Belper DE56 2JN. Tel: 0773 856040. Ladies Morris.

* Raddon Hill, Carolanne Brown, 7 Glenthorn Road, Exeter EX4 4QU. Tel: 0392 436002. Mixed Morris.

+ Rivington Ladies Morris, 61 Railway Road, Adlington, Chorley PR6 9QZ.

+ Royal Lancashire Morris, 93 Leverhouse Lane, Leyland, Preston PR5 2XP.

* Rumworth Morris of Bolton, Jim Fox, 3 Ashford Close, Harwood, Bolton BL2 3JY. Tel: 0204 305243. Men.

+ Rising Larks, Sue Curd, 25 Drake's Approach, West Clacton, Clacton CO15 2PX.

+ Royton Traditional Morris, Mike Higgins, 7 Cambridge Street, Royton, Oldham.

+ Risebridge Morris, Lesley Robinson, 44 Cromer Road, Hornchurch, Essex RM11 1EZ. Tel: 0402 441902.

+ Roughshod Clog, Sue Bearder, 18 Woodstock Lane, Avening, Tetbury, GL8 8NG. Tel: 0453 832370.

* Six Towns Morris, Sylvia Fisher, 12 Sefton Street, Etruria, Stoke on Trent ST1 4BQ. Tel: 0782 280849. Mixed.

* Spinning Jenny, Ann Dubaic, 7 Ollersett Lane, New Mills, Stockport SK12 4JE. Tel: 0663 742943. Ladies Step-dancers.

* Stafford Castle Clog Side, Kirsty Higgs, 63 Doxey Fields, Doxey, Stafford ST16 1HJ. Tel: 0785 45522. Mixed Step Dancers.

* Sun Oak, Kay Nightingale, 3 Byfleets Lane, Warnham, W. Sussex RH12 3RB. Tel: 0403 266086. Ladies Step-dancers.

* Sabotiers, June Martin, Dial Cottage, Mill Corner, Northiam, Rye TN31 6HU. Tel: 0797 2232. Mixed Step-dancers.

* Shuttlers Clog, Roger Howard, 6 Clifton Bank, Clifton, Buxton. Tel: 0298 77047. Mixed Step-dancers.

* Sowerby Bridge Morris Dancers, Fred Knights, 9 Bright Street, Sowerby Bridge, W. Yorks. Tel: 0422 831896. Men.

+ Sweet Coppin, D. & S.M. Rabson, Gerrans, Nynehead, Wellington TA21 0BS.

+ Singleton Cloggers, Maureen Smith, Todderstaffe Farm, Singleton, Poulton-le-Fylde, Blackpool. Mixed Morris.

* Saddleworth Morrismen, Richard Hankinson, 31 Moorgate Drive, Carr Brook, Stalybridge SK15 3LX. Tel: 0457 834871.

* Saddleworth Clog & Garland, Jo Walker, 8 Carr Drive, Milnrow, Rochdale OL16 3DX. Tel: 0706 523938. Ladies. Step-dancers.

+ Sticks & Steps, L. McGaw, 9 Woodbank Avenue, Offerton, Stockport SK1 4JL.

* Stockport Morrismen, Bill Fish, 54 Ludlow Road, Offerton, Stockport SK2 5BG. Tel: 061 480 5074.

+ Slubbing Billy's Mixed Morris, 52 Brougham Road, Marsden, Huddersfield HD7 JBJ.

+ Sheffield Celebrated Clog, Bev Popplewell, 121 Ringinglow Road, Sheffield S11 7PS.

+ St. Clemens Clogs, Mrs Wakeman, 24 Whitehill Road, Longfield, Kent DA3 7QS.

+ Sandgate Clog, Tony Murless, 119 High Street, Sandgate, Folkestone

+ Shanks Mare Morris, Eithne Brown, 20 Oak Dale Drive, Dun Laoghaire, Co. Dublin.

+ Soul Cake Clog, J.E. Braithwaite, Yew Tree Cottage, Church Street, Nunnington, Dover.

+ Southern Wood Clog, Norma Massey, Brookside, Checkley HR1 4ND

+ Spinning Jenny Clog, Rose Dorling, Church Road, Catsfield, Battle TN33 9DP. Tel: 0424 892417.

* Taeppas Tump, May Sommerville, 2 Crescent Drive, Maidenhead SL6 6AQ. Tel: 0628 29117. Ladies Morris.

* Treacle Eater Clog, Ms Phil Workman, 3 Mitchelmore Road, Yeovil. Tel: 0935 706287. Ladies Morris.

* Two Left Feet, Carol Lewis, 109 High Street, Pontardawe, W. Glamorgan. Tel: 0792 862172. Mixed. Step-dancers, Welsh style.

* Two by Two, Lynn Colbeck, 64 Greenfield Crescent, Cowplain, Waterlooville, Hants PO8 9EJ. Tel: 0705 599065. Mixed Step-dancers.

+ Tatterfoalls, Roberta Hindley, 3 West Common Lane, Scunthorpe.

* Turnberrie Castle, Linda Harris, Crispin House, 2 Crispin Lane, Thornbury, Bristol. Tel: 0454 413686. Ladies Morris. Stick & garland.

+ Three Shires, 6 Cobra Road, Sheffield S8 8QA.

+ Throstle's Nest, G. France, 4 Norfolk Road, Carlisle CA2 4JE.

* Terpsichore, Jacqui Green, 5 Hillcrest Close, Townville, Castleford WF10 3WS. Tel: 0977 510770. Mixed Morris.

* Ursa Major Ladies Morris, Wendy Crouch, 10 Butchers Close, Bishops Itchington, Warwicks CV33 0PX. Tel: 0926 613648.

* Wakefield Morris Dancers, Chris Walker, 20 Grove Road, Horbury, Wakefield WF4 6AQ. Tel: 0924 272183. Mixed or Ladies. The side is also known as Horberies Shroggies (Men) and The Ring O'Belles (Women).

* Women on the Wold, Judith Anderson, 99 Naunton Crescent, Cheltenham GL53 7BE. Tel: 0242 570561. Morris.

* Wessex Woods, Nikki White, 10 Old Wareham Road, Parkstone, Poole BH17 7NP. Tel: 0202 733699. Mixed. Step-dancers.

+ Whitworth Morrismen, Dave Robinson, 42 Crow Lane, Ramsbottom, Bury BL0 9BR.

+ Wrigley Head Morris, Chris Kelly, 87 Hay Street, Stalybridge SK15 2EH.

+ Westmorland Step & Garland, Anne Crawford, 17 Danes Road, Staveley, Kendal LA8 9PW.

+ White Thorn, Janet Jones, 6 Wood View Cottages, Vale Road, Chesham HP5 3NT.

+ Wimberry Clog, Ava Croxhall, Tiers Etat, Forest Patch, Christchurch, Coleford, Gloucs.

+ Whitchurch Clog, Gillian Aver, 44 Wickham Road, Holmer Green, High Wycombe.

* Whitehaven Academy, Neil Bettinson, 22 Main Street, St. Bees, Cumbria. Tel: 0946 823997. Mixed Step-dancers.

* Whitethorn Morris, Pat Collins, Flat 2, York Court, Bassett Road, Leighton Buzzard LU7 7LH. Tel: 0525 376699. Females.

* Yorkshire Rose, Elizabeth Titley, 6 Spring View, Luddendenfoot, Halifax HX2 6EX. Tel: 0442 883867. Mixed Step-dancers.

+ Yorkshire Chandelier, Anne Radford, 43 Tom Lane, Sheffield S10 3PA. Tel: 0742 301423.

Lastly, a tribute to *"Owd Cleverclogs"*, Sam Sherry (who, more than anyone, has been responsible for reviving interest in Lancashire-style clog dancing throughout the country) by Joe Wildman of Leigh.

Neaw Sam he were a champion dancer,
His fame it spread fer miles abeawt,
Monny's t'chap who challenged him,
Sam licked the lot witheawt a deawt.
Leet as fithers, were his dance steps,
Intricate an' hard t'perform,
Fast an' furious clattered th'irons,
Sam's flyin' feet danced up a storm.

> *Watch him dancin'*
> *Clitter, clatter,*
> *Polished clogs on flyin' feet,*
> *Heel an' toein'*
> *Left un, reet un,*
> *Mon, it is a gradely seet.*

He's even danced on th'idiots' lantern,
Traced his steps on t'telly screen,
Spindly shanks wi' movement blurrin',
T' best clog dancin' ever seen.
Sam's retired fro' competition
No moor does he dance up a storm,
Neaw he's teychyin' t' Lanky childer
Steps folk danced 'fore he were born.

> *Watch him dancin'*
> *Clitter, clatter,*
> *Steps an' reels on flyin' feet,*
> *Heel an' toein'*
> *Left un, reet un,*
> *Sparkin' irons on cobbled street.*

Come Sam, let's see thi clogs in action,
Dance just one moor time, owd lad,
Perform them steps as gi'ed thi fame,
Re-live again t'grand times tha's had.
Fer clogs are comin back in fashion
An' folk want t' larn heaw t' dance again,
So Sammy, teych 'em all tha knows
Yon irons play such a grand refrain.

> *Watch him dancin'*
> *Clitter, clatter,*
> *Flyin' feet on telly screen,*
> *Heel an' toein'*
> *Left un, reet un,*
> *Best clog dancin' ever seen.*